'Smart, entertaining and mov[...] is so glorious, beautiful and i[...]

'Always stimulating, this fine read gets you musing on your own desert island discs' *Mojo*

'Perceptive, funny, brought tears to my eyes' *Sunday Telegraph*

'A passionate defence of Hornby's taste, his writing and his success' *Literary Review*

'A book about the joy of listening to great pop songs, about the elusive genius of a catchy chorus … what shines most is Hornby himself – his wry self-awareness, his disarming honesty. Effortlessly readable, every chapter reminds us how special an observer of human behaviour Hornby is' *Heat*

'Sing along with him' *Arena*

'Chatty, confiding and unashamedly personal' *Harpers & Queen*

'Inspiring, amusing' *Rolling Stone*

'Anyone interested in great essays, or in the delicate art of being funny, or in how to write about one's feelings in such a way that other people will actually care … should love *31 Songs*' *San Francisco Chronicle*

'Conveys an irrepre[...] th[...] [...] the simple [...]nd superficial fun of hearing a gr[...]

'A wise book, conta[...] s[...] [...]

'Delivered in a huge[...] [...]oes in words what Hornby's tun[...] [...] good' *Time Out*

NICK HORNBY
31 songs

PENGUIN BOOKS

PENGUIN BOOKS

Published by the Penguin Group
Penguin Books Ltd, 80 Strand, London WC2R 0RL, England
Penguin Group (USA), Inc., 375 Hudson Street, New York, New York 10014, USA
Penguin Group (Canada), 90 Eglinton Avenue East, Suite 700, Toronto, Ontario, Canada M4P 2Y3
(a division of Pearson Penguin Canada Inc.)
Penguin Ireland, 25 St Stephen's Green, Dublin 2, Ireland (a division of Penguin Books Ltd)
Penguin Group (Australia), 250 Camberwell Road,
Camberwell, Victoria 3124, Australia (a division of Pearson Australia Group Pty Ltd)
Penguin Books India Pvt Ltd, 11 Community Centre,
Panchsheel Park, New Delhi – 110 017, India
Penguin Group (NZ), 67 Apollo Drive, Rosedale, North Shore 0632, New Zealand
(a division of Pearson New Zealand Ltd)
Penguin Books (South Africa) (Pty) Ltd, 24 Sturdee Avenue,
Rosebank, Johannesburg 2196, South Africa

Penguin Books Ltd, Registered Offices: 80 Strand, London WC2R 0RL, England

www.penguin.com

First published by Viking 2003
Published with additional material in Penguin Books 2003
Reissued with a revised 'Favourite Songs' section in Penguin Books 2011
1

Copyright © Nick Hornby, 2003, 2011
All rights reserved

The moral right of the author has been asserted

Three of the '31 Songs' included here first appeared, in different forms, in the following
publications: *Granta* ('I'm Like a Bird'); *Architectural Digest* ('First I Look at the Purse');
Idle Worship ('Mama You Been On My Mind'). The material published under 'and 14 albums'
was originally published in the *New Yorker*, 2000–2001

Designed by Smith & Gilmour, London
Printed in England by Clays Ltd, St Ives plc

ISBN: 978-0-241-95109-5

For Lee, and all the other people
who have introduced me to new songs.

Thanks to: Amanda Posey, Dave Eggers, Tony Lacey, Kle, Eli Horowitz and David Remnick.

Contents

31 songs

INTRODUCTION
Your Love Is The Place Where I Come From
Teenage Fanclub

So we were doing this thing, this launch party, for *Speaking with the Angel*, a book of short stories I put together to raise money for my son's school, and we – the school, the publishers of the book, me and my partner – were nervous about it. We didn't know if people would turn up, we didn't know whether the mix of readings and live music would work, we didn't know whether anyone would enjoy themselves. I arrived at the Hammersmith Palais early, and when I walked in I noticed two things simultaneously. One was that the venue looked great: there had been some big office party the night before, and there was all this glitter and tinsel everywhere; at the time, it seemed like a cheesy but effective way to symbolize magic. The other was that

Teenage Fanclub, who had agreed to play an acoustic set (and had postponed a gig in Europe so that they could do so), were going through a soundcheck. They were playing 'Your Love Is The Place Where I Come From', one of the loveliest songs on one of my favourite-ever albums, *Songs From Northern Britain*. It sounded great, a perfect musical expression of the tinsel; and I knew the moment I heard it that the evening, far from being a flop, would be special. And it was – it turned into one of the most memorable events with which I have been professionally connected.

Now, whenever I hear 'Your Love Is The Place Where I Come From', I think about that night, of course – how could it be otherwise? And initially, when I decided that I wanted to write a little book of essays about songs I loved (and that in itself was a tough discipline, because one has so many more opinions about what has gone wrong than about what is perfect), I presumed that the essays might be full of straightforward time-and-place connections like this, but they're not, not really. In fact, 'Your Love Is The Place Where I Come From' is just about the only one. And when I thought about why this should be so, why so few of the songs that are important to me come burdened with associative feelings or sensations, it occurred to me that the answer was obvious: if you love a song, love it enough for it to accompany you throughout the different stages of your life, then any specific memory is rubbed away by use. If I'd heard 'Thunder Road' in some girl's bedroom in 1975, decided that it was OK, and had never seen the girl or listened to the song much again, then hearing it now would probably bring back the smell of her underarm deodorant. But that isn't what happened; what happened was that I heard 'Thunder Road' and loved it, and I've listened to it at (alarmingly) frequent intervals ever since. 'Thunder Road' really only reminds me of itself, and, I suppose, of my life since I was eighteen – that is to say, of nothing much and too much.

There's this horrible song called (I think) 'Mummy I Want A Drink Of Water' that they used to play on a BBC children's radio show on Saturday morning; I don't think I've heard it since, but if I did it would remind me overwhelmingly of being a child and listening to the Saturday-morning children's radio show. There's a Gypsy Kings song that reminds me of being bombarded with plastic beer bottles at a football match in Lisbon, and several songs that remind me of college, or ex-girlfriends, or a summer job, but I don't own any of them – none of them means anything to me as music, just as memories, and I didn't want to write about memories. That wasn't the point. One can only presume that the people who say that their very favourite record of all time reminds them of their honeymoon in Corsica, or of their family chihuahua, don't actually like music very much. I wanted mostly to write about what it was in these songs that made me love them, not what I brought to the songs.

Songs are what I listen to, almost to the exclusion of everything else. I don't listen to classical music or jazz very often, and when people ask me what music I like, I find it very difficult to reply, because they usually want names of people, and I can only give them song titles. And mostly all I have to say about these songs is that I love them, and want to sing along to them, and force other people to listen to them, and get cross when these other people don't like them as much as I do; I'm sorry that I have nothing to say about 'Trampoline' by Joe Henry, or 'Stay' by Maurice Williams & the Zodiacs, or 'Help Me' by Sonny Boy Williamson, or 'Ms. Jackson' by Outkast, or anything by Lucinda Williams, or Marah, or Smokey Robinson, or Olu Dara, or the Pernice Brothers, or Ron Sexsmith, or about a thousand other people, including Marvin Gaye, for God's sake, nothing to say other than that they're all great and you should really hear them if you haven't already . . . I mean, I'm sure I could squeeze something out, and bump this book up to something like a regulation length in the process, but that wasn't the point either. Writers are always squeezing things out because books and articles are supposed to be a certain number of words, so you have in your hand the actual (i.e., natural, unforced, unpadded) shape of this particular book; it is, if you like, an organic book, raised without force-feeding or the assistance of steroids. And with organic stuff, you always have to pay more for less. Anyway . . .

Thunder Road
Bruce Springsteen

2

I can remember listening to this song and loving it in 1975; I can remember listening to this song and loving it almost as much quite recently, a few months ago. (And, yes, I was in a car, although I probably wasn't driving, and I certainly wasn't driving down any turnpike or highway or freeway, and the wind wasn't blowing through my hair, because I possess neither a convertible nor hair. It's not that version of Springsteen.) So I've loved this song for a quarter of a century now, and I've heard it more than anything else, with the possible exception of . . . Who am I kidding? There are no other contenders. See, what I was going to do there was soften the blow, slip in something black and/or cool (possibly 'Let's Get It On', which I think is the best pop record ever made, and which would easily make it into my top 20 most-played songs list, but not at number 2. Number 2 – and I'm trying to be honest here – would probably be something like '(White Man) In Hammersmith Palais' by The Clash, but it would be way, way behind. Let's say I've played 'Thunder Road' 1,500 times (just over once a week for twenty-five years, which sounds about right, if one takes into account the repeat plays in the first couple of years); '(White Man) . . .' would have clocked up something like 500 plays. In other words, there's no real competition.

It's weird to me how 'Thunder Road' has survived when so many other, arguably better songs – 'Maggie May', 'Hey Jude', 'God Save The Queen', 'Stir It Up', 'So Tired of Being Alone', 'You're A Big Girl Now' – have become less compelling as I've got older. It's not as if I can't see the flaws: 'Thunder Road' is overwrought, both lyrically (as Prefab Sprout pointed out, there's more to life than cars and girls, and surely the word 'redemption' is to be avoided like the plague when you're writing songs about redemption) and musically – after all, this four and three-quarter minutes provided Jim Steinman and Meatloaf with a whole career. It's also po-faced, in a way that Springsteen himself isn't, and if the doomed romanticism wasn't corny in 1975, then it certainly is now.

But sometimes, very occasionally, songs and books and films and pictures express who you are, perfectly. And they don't do this in words or images, necessarily; the connection is a lot less direct and more complicated than that. When I was first beginning to write seriously, I read Anne Tyler's *Dinner at the Homesick Restaurant*, and suddenly knew what I was, and what I wanted to be, for better or for worse. It's a process something like falling in love. You don't necessarily choose the best person, or the wisest, or the most beautiful; there's something else going on. There was a part of me that would rather have fallen for Updike, or Kerouac, or DeLillo – for someone masculine, at least, maybe somebody a little more opaque, and certainly someone who uses more swear-words – and, though I have admired those writers, at various stages in my life, admiration is a very different thing from the kind of transference I'm talking about. I'm talking about understanding – or at least feeling like I understand – every artistic decision, every impulse, the soul of both the work and its creator. 'This is me,' I wanted to say when I read Tyler's rich, sad, lovely novel. 'I'm not a character, I'm nothing like the author, I haven't had the experiences she writes about. But even so, this is what I feel like, inside. This is what I would sound like, if ever I were to find a voice.' And I did find a voice, eventually, and it was mine, not hers; but never-theless, so powerful was the process of identification that I still don't feel as though I've expressed myself as well, as completely, as Tyler did on my behalf then.

So, even though I'm not American, no longer young, hate cars, and can recognize why so many people find Springsteen bombastic and histrionic (but not why they find him macho or jingoistic or dumb – that kind of ignor-ant judgement has plagued Springsteen for a huge part of his career, and is made by smart people who are actually a lot dumber than he has ever been), 'Thunder Road' somehow manages to speak for me. This is partly – and perhaps shamingly – because a lot of Springsteen's songs from this period are about becoming famous, or at least achieving some kind of public validation through his art: what else are we supposed to think when the last line of the song is 'I'm pulling out of here to win', other than that he has won, simply by virtue of playing the song, night after night after night, to an ever-increasing crowd of people? (And what else are we supposed to think when in 'Rosalita' he sings, with a touching, funny and innocent glee, 'Cos the record company, Rosie, just gave me a big advance', other than that the record company has just given him a big advance?) It's never objectionable or obnoxious, this dream of fame, because it derives from a restless and uncontrollable artistic urge – he knows he has talent to burn, and the proper reward for this, he seems to suggest, would be the financial wherewithal to fulfil it – rather than an interest in celebrity for its own sake. Hosting a TV quiz show, or assassinating a president, wouldn't scratch the itch at all.

And, of course – don't let anyone tell you otherwise – if you have dreams of becoming a writer, then there are murky, mucky visions of fame attached to these dreams too; 'Thunder Road' was my answer to every rejection letter I received, and every doubt expressed by friends or relatives. They lived in towns for losers, I told myself, and I, like Bruce, was pulling out of there to win. (These towns, incidentally, were Cambridge – full of loser doctors and lawyers and academics – and London – full of loser successes of every description – but never mind. This was the material I had to work with, and work with it I did.)

It helped a great deal that, as time went by, and there was no sign of me pulling out of anywhere to do anything very much, and certainly not with the speed implied in the song, 'Thunder Road' made reference to age, thus accommodating this lack of forward momentum. 'So you're scared and you're thinking that maybe we ain't that young any more', Bruce sang, and that line worked for me even when I had begun to doubt whether there was any magic in the night: I continued thinking I wasn't that young any more for a long, long time – decades, in fact – and even today I choose to interpret it as a wistful observation of middle age, rather than the sharp fear that comes on in late youth.

It also helped that, some time in the early to mid-eighties, I came across another version of the song, a bootleg studio recording of Springsteen alone with an acoustic guitar (it's on *War And Roses*, the *Born To Run* outtakes bootleg); he reimagines 'Thunder Road' as a haunting, exhausted hymn to the past, to lost love and missed opportunities and self-delusion and bad luck and failure, and that worked pretty well for me, too. In fact, when I try to hear that last line of the song in my head, it's the acoustic version that comes first. It's slow, and mournful, and utterly convincing: an artist who can persuade you of the truth of what he is singing with either version is an artist who is capable of an awful lot.

There are other bootleg versions that I play and love. One of the great things about the song as it appears on *Born To Run* is that those first few bars, on wheezy harmonica and achingly pretty piano, actually sound like they refer to something that has already happened before the beginning of the record, something momentous and sad but not destructive of all hope; as 'Thunder Road' is the first track on side one of *Born To Run*, the album begins, in effect, with its own closing credits. In performance at the end of the seventies, during the Darkness on the Edge of Town tour, Springsteen maximized this effect by seguing into 'Thunder Road' out of one of his bleakest, most desperate songs, 'Racing In The Street', and the harmonica that marks the transformation of one song into the other feels like a sudden and glorious hint of spring after a long, withering winter. On the bootlegs of those seventies shows, 'Thunder Road' can finally provide the salvation that its position on *Born To Run* denied it.

Maybe the reason 'Thunder Road' has sustained for me is that, despite its energy and volume and fast cars and hair, it somehow manages to sound elegiac, and the older I get the more I can hear that. When it comes down to it, I suppose that I too believe that life is momentous and sad but not destructive of all hope, and maybe that makes me a self-dramatizing depressive, or maybe it makes me a happy idiot, but either way 'Thunder Road' knows how I feel and who I am, and that, in the end, is one of the consolations of art.

Postscript

A few years ago, I started to sell a lot of books, at first only in the UK, and then later in other countries too, and to my intense bewilderment found that I had somehow become part of the literary and cultural mainstream. It wasn't something I had expected, or was prepared for. Although I could see no reason why anyone would feel excluded from my work – it wasn't like it was difficult, or experimental – my books still seemed to me to be quirky and small-scale. But suddenly all sorts of people, people I didn't know or like or respect, had opinions about me and my work, which overnight seemed to go from being fresh and original to clichéd and ubiquitous, without a word of it having changed. And I was shown this horrible reflection of myself and what I did, a funfair hall-of-mirrors reflection, all squidged-up and distorted – me, but not me. It wasn't like I was given a particularly hard time, and certainly other people, some of whom I know, have experienced much worse. But even so, it becomes in those circumstances very hard to hang on to the idea of what you want to do.

And yet Springsteen somehow managed to find a way through. His name is still taken in vain frequently (a year or so ago I read a newspaper piece attacking Tony Blair for his love of Bruce, an indication, apparently, of the Prime

Minister's incorrigible philistinism), and for some, the hall-of-mirrors reflection is the only Springsteen they can see. He went from being rock 'n' roll future to a lumpy, flag-waving, stadium-rocking meathead in the space of a few months, again with nothing much having changed, beyond the level of his popularity. Anyway, his strength of purpose, and the way he has survived the assault on his sense of self, seem to me exemplary; sometimes it's hard to remember that a lot of people liking what you do doesn't necessarily mean that what you do is of no value whatsoever. Indeed, sometimes it might even suggest the opposite.

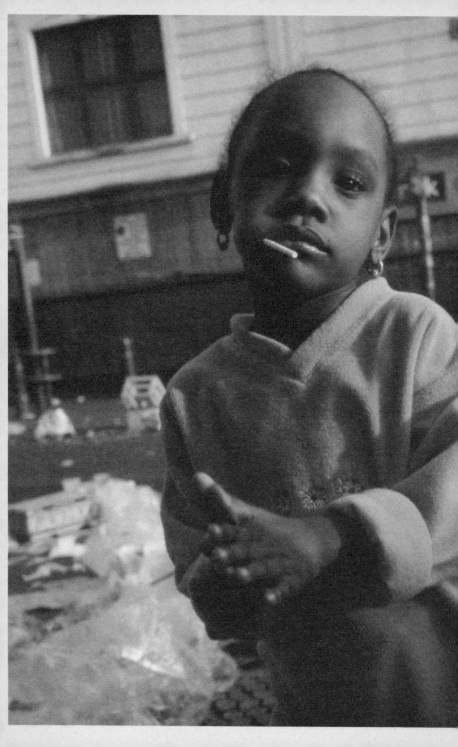

3
I'm Like a Bird
Nelly Furtado

Oh, of course I can understand people dismissing pop music. I know that a lot of it, nearly all of it, is trashy, unimaginative, poorly written, slickly produced, inane, repetitive and juvenile (although at least four of these adjectives could be used to describe the incessant attacks on pop that you can still find in posh magazines and newspapers); I know too, believe me, that Cole Porter was 'better' than Madonna or Travis, that most pop songs are aimed cynically at a target audience three decades younger than I am, that in any case the golden age was thirty-five years ago and there has been very little of value since. It's just that there's this song I heard on the radio, and I bought the CD, and now I have to hear it ten or fifteen times a day . . .

That's the thing that puzzles me about those who feel that contemporary pop (and I use the word to encompass soul, reggae, country, rock – anything and everything that might be regarded as trashy) is beneath them, or behind them, or beyond them – some preposition denoting distance, anyway: does this mean that you never hear, or at least never enjoy, new songs, that everything you whistle or hum was written years, decades, centuries ago? Do you really deny yourselves the pleasure of mastering a tune (a pleasure, incidentally, that your generation is perhaps the first in the history of mankind to forgo) because you are afraid it might make you look as if you don't know who Harold Bloom is? Wow. I'll bet you're fun at parties.

The song that has been driving me pleasurably potty recently is 'I'm Like a Bird' by Nelly Furtado. Only history will judge whether Ms Furtado turns out to be any kind of artist, and though I have my suspicions that she will not change the way we look at the world, I can't say that I'm very bothered: I will always be grateful to her for creating in me the narcotic need to hear her song again and again. It is, after all, a harmless need, easily satisfied, and there are few enough of those in the world. I don't even want to make a case for this song, as opposed to any other – although I happen to think that it's a very good pop song, with a dreamy languor and a bruised optimism that immediately distinguishes it from its anaemic and stunted peers. The point is that a few months ago it didn't exist, at least as far as we are concerned, and now here it is, and that, in itself, is a small miracle.

Dave Eggers has a theory that we play songs over and over, those of us who do, because we have to 'solve' them, and it's true that in our early relationship with, and courtship of, a new song, there is a stage which is akin to a sort of emotional puzzlement. There's a little bit in 'I'm

Like a Bird', for example, about halfway through, where
the voice is double-tracked on a phrase, and the effect –
especially on someone who is not a musician, someone
who loves and appreciates music but is baffled and seduced
by even the simplest musical tricks – is rich and fresh
and addictive.

Sure, it will seem thin and stale soon enough. Before
very long I will have 'solved' 'I'm Like a Bird', and I won't
want to hear it very much any more – a three-minute pop
song can only withhold its mysteries for so long, after
all. So, yes, it's disposable, as if that makes any difference
to anyone's perceptions of the value of pop music. But
then, shouldn't we be sick of '*Moonlight*' *Sonata* by now?
Or *Christina's World*? Or *The Importance of Being Earnest*?
They're empty! Nothing left! We sucked 'em dry! That's
what gets me: the very people who are snotty about the
disposability of pop will go over and over again to see
Lady Bracknell say 'A handbag?' in a funny voice. They
don't think that joke's exhausted itself? Maybe disposability is a sign of pop music's maturity, a recognition
of its own limitations, rather than the converse. And
anyway, I was sitting in a doctor's waiting-room the other
day, and four little Afro-Caribbean girls, patiently sitting
out their mother's appointment, suddenly launched into

Nelly Furtado's song. They were word-perfect, and they had a couple of dance moves, and they sang with enormous appetite and glee, and I liked it that we had something in common, temporarily; I felt as though we all lived in the same world, and that doesn't happen so often.

A couple of times a year I make myself a tape to play in the car, a tape full of all the new songs I've loved over the previous few months, and every time I finish one I can't believe that there'll be another. Yet there always is, and I can't wait for the next one; you need only a few hundred more things like that, and you've got a life worth living.

4 Heartbreaker
Led Zeppelin

The traditional interpretation of boys and their infatuation with heavy (or nu-, or rap) metal involves guitars that serve as substitutes for the penis, homo-eroticism, and all sorts of other things betokening perversity, sexual confusion and intractable, morbid neuroses. True, I spent a brief period in love with the Irish blues-rock guitarist Rory Gallagher (unrequited); and true, I would, for the first three or four years of my life as a rock fan, only listen to singers who would happily admit to eating rodents and/or reptiles. And yet I suspect that there is a musical, rather than patho-logical, explanation for my early dalliance with Zeppelin and Sabbath and Deep Purple, namely that I was unable to trust my judgement of a song. Like a pretentious but dim adult who won't watch a film unless it has subtitles, I wouldn't listen to anything that wasn't smothered in loud, distorted electric guitars. How was I to know whether the music was any good otherwise? Songs that were played on piano, or acoustic guitar, by people without moustaches and beards (girls, for example), people who ate salad rather than rodents . . . well, that could be bad music, trying to play a trick on me. That could be people pretending to be The Beatles when they weren't. How would I know, if it was all undercover like that? No, best avoid the whole question of good or bad and stick to loud instead. You couldn't go too wrong with loud.

The titles helped, too. Song titles which did not contain obvious heavy-rock signifiers were like music without loud guitars: somebody might be trying to part you from your pocket money, fool you into thinking it was something it wasn't. Look at, say, *Blue*, by Joni Mitchell. Well, I did, hard, and I didn't trust it. You could easily imagine a bad song called 'My Old Man' (not least because my dad liked a song called 'My Old Man's A Dustman') or 'Little Green' (not least because my dad liked a song called 'Little Green Apples'); and God knows you couldn't tell whether the record was any good by listening to the fucking thing. But the songs on Black Sabbath's album *Paranoid*, for example, were solid, dependable, immediately indicative of quality. How could there be a bad song called 'Iron Man', or 'War Pigs', or – my cup ranneth over – 'Rat Salad'?

So for me, learning to love quieter songs – country, soul and folk songs, ballads sung by women and played on the piano or the viola or some damned thing, songs with harmonies and titles like 'Carey' (because who with a pair of ears that work doesn't love *Blue*?) – is not about getting older, but about acquiring a musical confidence, an ability to judge for myself. Sometimes it seems that, with each passing year, a layer of grungy guitar has been scraped away, until eventually I have reached the stage where I can, I hope, tell a good George Jones song from a bad one. Songs undressed like that, without a stitch of Stratocaster on them, are scary – you have to work them out for yourself.

And then, once you are able to do that, you become as lazy and as afraid of your own judgement as you were when you were fourteen. How do you tell whether a CD is any good? You look for evidence of quiet good taste, is how. You look for a moody black-and-white cover, evidence of violas, maybe a guest appearance from someone classy, some ironic song titles, a sticker with a quote taken from a review in *Mojo* or a broadsheet newspaper, perhaps a couple of references somewhere to literature or cinema. And, of course, you stop listening to music made by shrieking, leather-trousered, shaggy-haired men altogether. Because how are you supposed to know whether it's any good or not, when it's played that loud, by people apparently so hostile to the aesthetics of understated modernity?

I discovered, some time during the last few years, that my musical diet was light on carbohydrates, and that the rock riff is nutritionally essential – especially in cars and on book tours, when you need something quick and cheap to get you through a long day. Nirvana, *The Bends* and The Chemical Brothers restimulated my appetite, but only Led Zeppelin could satisfy it; in fact, if I ever had to hum a blues-metal riff to a puzzled alien, I'd choose Zeppelin's 'Heartbreaker', from *Led Zeppelin II*. I'm not sure that me going 'DANG DANG DANG DANG DA-DA-DANG, DA-DA-DA-DA-DA DANG DANG DA-DA-DANG' would enlighten him especially, but I'd feel that I'd done as good a job as the circumstances allowed. Even written down like that (albeit with upper-case assistance), it seems to me that the glorious, imbecilic loudness of the track is conveyed effectively and unambiguously. Read it again. See? It rocks.

The thing I like most about rediscovering Led Zeppelin – and listening to The Chemical Brothers, and *The Bends* – is that they can no longer be comfortably accommodated into my life. So much of what you consume when you get older is about accommodation: I have kids, and neighbours, and a partner who could quite happily never hear another blues-metal riff or block-rockin' beat in her life; I have less time, less tolerance for bullshit, more interest in good taste, more confidence in my own judgement. The culture with which I surround myself is a reflection of my personality and the circumstances of my life, which is in part how it should be. In learning to do that, however, things get lost, too, and one of the things that got lost – along with a taste for, I don't know, hospital dramas involving sick children, and experimental films – was Jimmy Page. The noise he makes is not who I am any more, but it's still a noise worth listening to; it's also a reminder that the attempt to grow up smart comes at a cost.

One Man Guy
Rufus Wainwright

5

I try not to believe in God, of course, but sometimes things happen in music, in songs, that bring me up short, make me do a double-take. When things add up to more than the sum of their parts, when the effects achieved are inexplicable, then atheists like me start to get into difficult territory. Take Rufus Wainwright's version of his father Loudon's 'One Man Guy', for example. There should be nothing evoking the spirit about it, really: the song's lovely, but it's a little sour, a little sad, jokey – the joke being that the song is not about the joys of monogamy but is about the joys of solipsism and misanthropy, a joke that is given a neat little twist by Wainwright junior's sexual orientation – and it's hard to imagine that God has time to pay a visit to something so wry and so self-mocking. And yet, weirdly, He does. There's no doubt about it. (And, of course, in doing so, He answers once and for all the question of what

He thinks of homosexuality: he's not bothered one way or the other. Official.)

For me, He comes in at the beginning of the second verse, just when Rufus and his sister Martha begin to harmonize. Perhaps significantly (or perhaps He is merely demonstrating a hitherto unsuspected sense of humour), His presence first makes itself known on the line 'People meditate, hey, that's just great, trying to find the Inner You'. It's the harmony that does it, although whether that's cause or effect is a moot point. Does God come in because Martha and Rufus are singing so beautifully together – does He hear it from afar and think, 'Hey, that's My kind of music, and I'm going to see what's going on'? Or does He enable them to sing together – does He spot what they're pitching for and help them along the way?

When I say that you can hear God in 'One Man Guy' by Rufus Wainwright, I do not mean to suggest that there is an old chap with a beard – a divine Willie Nelson, if you will – warbling along with them. Nor do I wish to imply that this surprise guest appearance at the beginning of the second verse proves that Jesus died for our sins, or that rich men will have difficulty entering the Kingdom of Heaven. I just mean that at certain spine-shivering musical moments – and you will have your own, inevitably – it becomes difficult to remain a literalist. (I have no such difficulty when I hear religious music, by the way, no matter how beautiful. They're cheating, those composers: they're inviting Him in, egging Him on, and surely He wouldn't fall for that? I think He'd have enough self-respect to stay well away.)

I'm not sure what difference it makes to me, this occasional vision of the Divine in the music I love. OK, maybe it comes as a relief, because a lot of people I have a lot of time for, writers and musicians and sports stars and politicians, have a great deal to say on the subject of God, and hitherto I had felt a bit left out; now I have something, a little scrap of spirituality, I can wave back at them. Oh, and as a writer, I don't normally have much patience for the ineffable – I ought to think that everything's effing effable, otherwise what's the point? But I'm not sure there are words to describe what happens when two voices mesh (and isn't the power and beauty and sheer perfection of a simple chord a bit, you know, Outer Limits? It's no wonder Pythagoras got so worked up about harmony). All I can say is that I can hear things that aren't there, see and feel things I can't normally see and feel, and start to realize that, yes, there is such a thing as an immortal soul, or, at the very least, a unifying human consciousness, that our lives are short but have meaning. Beyond that, I'm not sure it changes very much, really. I'm not going to listen to stuff like this too often, though, just in case.

Samba Pa Ti
Santana

6

'Samba Pa Ti' is an instrumental, rather than a song, but for a crucial period in my mid-teens, when I first came across it, it spoke to me as eloquently as anything that contained lyrics: I was convinced that it described sex. More specifically, 'Samba Pa Ti' was what I was going to hear when I lost my virginity – if not on the stereo, then in my head. It starts off slow and mysterious and beautiful, and then it gets more urgent, and then – well, then it fades out. (The track lasts four minutes and forty-seven seconds, incidentally; but before I am accused of showing off, I had anticipated that we'd be doing other things – kissing, getting undressed, possibly waiting for a bus home from the cinema – during the slow bit, so I was confident that I could make it through to the fade.)

I hadn't, at that time, heard anything that would serve as a better soundtrack; indeed, I'm not entirely sure that I've heard anything to beat it since. All sorts of pieces of music are constantly being described as 'sexy', but that doesn't necessarily mean that you'd want them to accompany love-making. Most of them, in fact, are sexual substitutes, rather than sexual accompaniments – music for people who aren't getting any (or won't be until they get home) rather than people who are. Would it be possible to fuck to the tune of 'Let's Get It On' without laughing? (Not that there's anything wrong with laughing during sex, but laughter was not, I suspect, the sound that Marvin intended to provoke. If you want to laugh, then why not enhance your amorous pleasure with 'I Have a Pony', by Steven Wright, or 'Disco Duck', by Rick Dees?) And even if you did manage to get through it without a giggling fit, could you manage the same during 'If I Should Die Tonight', the third track on the album? Granted, you may have finished by then, but there's every chance that you won't have turned the music off, which means that you'll be lying there with your girlfriend, or boyfriend, or someone you don't know very well, while Marvin is telling you that the sex you have just had is unlikely to be bettered during the remainder of your lifetimes – indeed, that you may as well shuffle off this mortal coil now, so anticlimactic is any subsequent experience likely to be. This is an intolerable burden to place on any couple, and certainly inhibits the usual post-coital activities (sleep, the hunt for socks or the TV remote, exchanges of false email addresses, etc.).

Prince's 'Do Me, Baby', from the *Controversy* album, is one of the most sexually explicit, and genuinely erotic, records ever made, but it's every bit as problematic as 'Let's Get It On'. For a start, there's a bit after the climax (crashing piano chords, moans, sighs, and so on) when he goes all weird, and starts saying he's 'soooo cold', which might well prove to be something of a distraction unless you too have an inappropriately undertogged duvet. And though the next song on the album, 'Private Joy', is hardly what you want to hear at an intimate moment, at least it brings the first side of *Controversy* to a close if you have the album on vinyl; if you have the CD, however, you may find your-self in the unhappy position of trying to give and receive carnal pleasure while Prince sings 'Ronnie Talk To Russia' – a sentiment that no longer even contains the virtue, arguable in a sexual context anyway, of urgency. What, one wonders, was he thinking of when he sequenced the tracks? Presumably something along the lines of, 'Give them five minutes to get their breath back, and then they'll be wanting to think about impending Armageddon.'

Inevitably, I did not lose my virginity to 'Samba Pa Ti'. Instead, my unfortunate girlfriend and I were listening to the second side of Rod Stewart's *Smiler*, my favourite record at the time; side two, I notice now, features 'Hard Road', 'I've Grown Accustomed To Her Face' and 'Dixie Toot'. In a perfect world, obviously, that wouldn't have happened.

7

Mama You Been On My Mind
Rod Stewart

We were listening to the second side of *Smiler* because I was, in my mid-to-late teens, a huge Rod Stewart fan. It's hard to imagine now, but loving Rod Stewart in 1973 was the equivalent of loving Oasis in 1994, or The Stone Roses in 1989 – in other words, although it didn't make you the coolest kid in your class, it was certainly nothing to be ashamed of. One of the best things about Cameron Crowe's film *Almost Famous* is that it recognizes this, gives Rod his due; when the band pulls away in the bus, it's 'Every Picture Tells A Story' they're all listening to. It's just about the only evidence for the defence that I have at my disposal now, because within a few years there was plenty to be ashamed of: Britt Ekland, for example. And several other interchangeably blonde women who weren't Britt Ekland but may as well have been. And 'Do Ya Think I'm Sexy'. And 'Ole Ola', the 1978 Scotland World Cup song (the chorus of which went 'Ole ole, ole ola / We're going to bring the World Cup back from over thar'). And his obsession with LA, and the champagne and straw boaters on album sleeves, and the drawing on the cover of *Atlantic Crossing*, and the Faces' live album (on which the last thing you hear at the end of side two is Stewart saying, with a nasty leer, 'Thank you for your time . . . and your money'), and the all-purpose, session-musician, sub-Stones plod-rock that can be found on any of his post-Faces work, 'Hot Legs' being the template . . . 'Now there's a man who's never let you down,' a friend remarked dryly when I once confessed my soft spot, and it's true that Rod's record is not without its blemishes.

And yet I owe him a great deal. His first four or five solo albums contained the first ballads that I ever loved – 'Country Comfort', 'Tomorrow Is A Long Time', 'Handbags And Gladrags', 'Reason To Believe', 'I'd Rather Go Blind', loads of them – and I'd still rather listen to a ballad than anything else. And he was the first singer to teach me that there was an art to interpretation: his best songs were invariably covers, and I had always presumed (I was a music snob even before I knew anything) that covers were inauthentic, somehow, and inevitably inferior – that only the originals really counted. But when I checked out these originals, I discovered to my confusion that quite often he had improved upon them. Obviously he wasn't a better singer than Sam Cooke, but Stewart's take on 'Bring It On Home To Me' had a raucousness and a swing that I couldn't hear in Cooke's version; and Dylan's 'Mama You Been On My Mind' seems to me to be not much more than a strum – an exquisite strum, with one of Dylan's loveliest and simplest lyrics, but a strum nonetheless. Stewart's evident love for the song rescues it, or at least spotlights it: where Dylan almost throws it away, with the implication that there's plenty more where that one came from, Stewart's reverence seems to dignify it, invest it with an epical quality Dylan denies it. I probably like both versions equally now, but if it hadn't been for Stewart, I'd never have been able to spot that there was anything there.

These are the records I own because of Rod Stewart: Bobby Bland's *His California Album*, from which Stewart borrowed 'It's Not The Spotlight' (and, though the cover is flatter and less piquant, Rod judiciously elected to leave out Bland's really rather unpleasant phlegm-clearing gargles); my entire Bobby Womack collection (Stewart never, as far as I know, attempted a Womack song, but he ripped a couple of them off, and always talked about Womack in interviews); Chuck Berry's *Golden Decade*, the Temptations' *Greatest Hits*, Sam Cooke's *Golden Greats*. I was introduced to The Isley Brothers ('This Old Heart Of Mine'), Aretha Franklin ('(You Make Me Feel) Like a Natural Woman/ Man') and Crazy Horse ('I Don't Want To Talk About It'). And once I knew about Aretha and Bobby Bland and the Temptations, I was led on to B.B. King and the Four Tops and Atlantic, and Chess, and . . . This is all pretty good stuff; I would hate not to have discovered it when I did. If I'd been similarly smitten by Elton John or Jethro Tull or Mike Oldfield, all of whom were competing for my attention at around the same time, it's possible that I might not be listening to music now.

Because the people who stick with pop music the longest, it seems to me, are those who entrust themselves at a tender age to somebody like Stewart, somebody who was clearly a fan himself. Those who fell for The Stones got to hear, if they could be bothered, Arthur Alexander and Solomon Burke and Don Covay (and anyone who likes Jagger and has yet to hear Covay should check him out – you'd be amused, unless you have too much invested in Jagger being a true original). Zeppelin fans might have been moved to seek out Muddy Waters and Howlin' Wolf. The antecedents of Yes and Genesis were Pink Floyd, and before that nobody much, really, and that was, in retrospect, part of the reason I didn't like them very much. The music felt airless and synthetic, and it seemed even then as if all the prog rockers would rather have been classical musicians, as if pop were beneath them, somehow. They led you up a blind alley; there was nowhere to go.

Recently Elvis Costello, another old Rod Stewart fan, offered to produce him, and thus offer him a route to redemption. I have the same fantasy. I'd like to choose the songs (I've got a couple of ideas, but they're trade secrets, obviously) and a sympathetic band, a group of musicians who could approximate that ramshackle folky stomp on 'Every Picture Tells A Story' . . . I reckon I'd get some pretty good work out of him. Maybe Elvis and I could work together, although he'd have to do most of the knob-twiddling. I'm not very good at that. On the other hand, why should Rod bother? He's done OK without us.

8

Can You Please Crawl Out Your Window?
Bob Dylan

9 Rain
The Beatles

By expressing no preference between a Rod Stewart version of a Bob Dylan song and the Dylan original, I have, I know, exposed myself: I'm not a big Dylan fan. I've got *Blonde On Blonde* and *Highway 61 Revisited*, obviously. And *Bringing It All Back Home* and *Blood On the Tracks*. Anyone who likes music owns those four. And I'm interested enough to have bought *The Bootleg Series Volumes 1–3*, and that live album we now know wasn't recorded at the Royal Albert Hall. The reviews of *Time Out Of Mind* and *Love And Theft* convinced me to shell out for these two, as well, although I can't say I listen to them very often. I once asked for *Biograph* as a birthday present, so with that and *The Bootleg Series* I've got two Dylan boxed sets. I also, now I look, seem to own copies of *World Gone Wrong, The Basement Tapes* and *Good As I Been To You*, although this, I suspect, is due more to my respect for Greil Marcus, who has written so persuasively and brilliantly about Dylan's folk and blues roots, than to my Dylanphilia. And I have somehow picked up along the way *Street Legal*, *Desire*, and *John Wesley Harding*. Oh, and I bought *Oh Mercy* because it contains the lovely 'Most of the Time', which is on the *High Fidelity* soundtrack. There are, therefore, around twenty separate Bob Dylan CDs on my shelf; in fact I own more recordings by Dylan than by any other artist. Some people – my mother, say, who may not own twenty CDs in total – would say that I am a Dylan fanatic, but I know Dylan fanatics, and they would not recognize me as one of them. (I have a friend who stays logged on to the Dylan website Expecting Rain most of the day at work – as if the website were CNN and Dylan's career were the Middle East – and who owns 130 Dylan albums, including a fourteen-CD box of every single thing Dylan recorded during 1965 apart from – get this – *Highway 61 Revisited*, the only thing he recorded during 1965 that sane people would want to own. He's pretty keen.) I can't quote whole songs – just the odd line here and there. I do not regard Dylan as any more important, or any more talented, than Elvis Presley, or Marvin Gaye, or Bob Marley, or several other major artists. I have no opinion as to whether he was a poet, and especially not as to whether he was a better poet than another poet, I don't own any bootlegs, I have no desire to see him play live again (I saw him twice, and that was more than enough), I have no theories about any single song . . . I just like some of the tunes, and that, I have been led to believe, is Not Good Enough.

There is a very clever English artist called Emma Kay who has done a series of artworks which consist entirely of her (verbal) memories of Shakespeare plays. If I were to do the same for the life of Bob Dylan, it would consist of the following list:

Zimmerman

Hibbing, Minnesota

New York coffee houses

Joan Baez (But what about her? I'm not sure.)

The Band, formerly The Hawks. Electricity. 'Judas!'

Motorbike crash. Never as good afterwards. (Is that true? I fear I may be getting the crash confused with Elvis's spell in the army.)

Sara (Sara who? Don't know). Divorce.

Eye-liner

Christianity

Farm Aid

Lots of tours

This, it seems to me, is way too much knowledge. (Why on earth am I able to name his home town? And why should I recall that he fell off his bloody motorbike?) I will not attempt a similar list pertaining to the life of William Shakespeare, because it would be far too shaming, but suffice to say that it would not extend much beyond Stratford-upon-Avon, Anne Hathaway and her cottage, the Globe and the Dark Lady. Jane Austen: Bath; unmarried; once went to my sister's house, apparently, although some time before my sister moved there. (That must be right, mustn't it, dates-wise?) Obviously I have no one but myself to blame for my ignorance of our major literary figures. I'm not responsible for my intimacy with the Life of Bob, however. That's the fault of all sorts of other people: friends, music writers, university professors, editors at my publishing house. He's hard to avoid – mostly because his status as a major poet allows one to like him without inducing the feelings of intellectual insecurity that usually accompany devotion to a pop star. I suppose I resent that. In my book, you're either in or you're out, and if you're in, then get in properly, and find as big a place in your heart for the stupid stuff – 'Mmmm Bop' and 'Judy Is a Punk' – as for the stuff that you can pass off as poetry. Obviously I wouldn't ask you to find as big a place in your head for 'Mmmm Bop', but then, that's partly the trouble: the best music connects to the soul, not the brain, and I worry that all this Dylan-devotion is somehow anti-music – that it tells us the heart doesn't count, and only the head matters.

Elsewhere in this book you will find fanciful comparisons between literature and music, specifically novels and songs, but you sure can exhaust a great song much more quickly than you can clean out a great novel, and – partly, I suspect, because I am not interested in Dylan as poet – I've exhausted Bob, or at least the bits of Bob that I'm interested in. I wish I hadn't; there's a density and a gravity to a Dylan song that you can't find anywhere else. But even more than I regret mining the seam for all it's worth (or all it's worth to me), I regret never having heard any of the songs at the right age, in the right year. What must it have been like, to listen to 'Like A Rolling Stone' in 1966, aged nineteen or twenty? I heard 'White Riot' and 'Anarchy In The UK' in 1976, aged nineteen, but the enormous power those records had then has mostly been lost now. Much of the shock came from their volume and speed and brevity, and records consequently became louder and faster and shorter; listening to them a quarter of a century later is like watching old film of Jesse Owens running. You can see that he won his races, but all sense of pace has been wiped away by Maurice Greene. 'Like A Rolling Stone', however, still sounds perfect. It just doesn't sound fresh any more. In Victorian London they used to burn phosphorus at seances in an attempt to see ghosts, and I suspect that the pop-music equivalent is our obsession with B-sides and alternative versions and unreleased material. If you can hear Dylan and The Beatles being unmistakably themselves at their peak – but unmistakably themselves in a way we haven't heard a thousand, a million times before – then suddenly you get a small but thrilling flash of their spirit, and it's as close as we'll ever get, those of us born in the wrong time, to knowing what it must have been like to have those great records burst out of the radio at you when you weren't expecting them, or anything like them. 'Can You Please Crawl Out Your Window?' is, I accept, a minor Dylan track, one of his snarly (and less than poetic) put-downs, but it is from my favourite period (electric, with that crisp, clean organ sound), and I haven't heard it a million times before, so it sneaks its way on to car tapes now. And 'Rain' is a great Beatles song from a great year in their career, the year that Oasis have been trying to live in for the last ten years, and it's wonderful to listen to a Lennon/McCartney song that hasn't quite had all the pulp sucked from it. I'll get sick of both these songs in the end, of course – they just don't last long enough to keep their mystery and magic for ever. But they'll do for now.

10

You Had Time
Ani DiFranco

I've Had It
Aimee Mann

11

You'd think that self-reflective songs about the music-biz life – about the pain and joy of being a talented but struggling singer-songwriter ('I've Had It'), or about the difficulty of maintaining a relationship and a career in rock 'n' roll ('You Had Time') – would suck. You'd think that these songs would reek of self-indulgence, or betoken a failure of imagination and creativity and empathy; you'd think that DiFranco and Mann are three-quarters of the way down the road that leads to songs about room service, concession stands and the imbecility of local-radio presenters. So how are these two of the most moving and beautiful pieces of music one could hope to come across on pop albums?

'You Had Time' sets itself a further handicap: it begins with more than two minutes of apparently hopeful and occasionally discordant piano noodling. I know, I know –

neither 'Baby Let's Play House' nor '(Hit Me) Baby One More Time' begins with piano noodling, and they wouldn't have been much good if they had; that's not what pop is supposed to be about. But DiFranco's song is nothing if not ambitious, because what it does – or, at any rate, what it pretends to do – is describe the genesis of its own creation: it shows its workings, in a way that would delight any maths teacher. When it kicks off, the noodling sounds impressionistic, like a snatch of soundtrack for an arty but emotional film – maybe *Don't Look Now*, because the piano has a sombre, churchy feel to it, and you can imagine Donald Sutherland and Julie Christie wandering around Venice in the cold, grieving and doomed. But it cheers up a little, when DiFranco makes out that she's suddenly hit upon the gorgeous little riff that gives the song its spine. She's not quite there yet, because she hasn't found anything to do with her left hand, so there's a little bit more messing about; and then, as if by magic (although of course we know that it's merely the magic of hard work and talent) she works out a counterpoint, and she's there. Indeed, she celebrates the birth of the song by shoving the piano out of the way and playing the song proper on acoustic guitar – the two instruments are fused together with a deliberately improbable seamlessness on the recording, as if she wants us to see this as a metaphor for the creative process, rather than as the creative process itself. It's a sweet idea, a fan's dream of how music is created; I'd love to be a musician precisely because a part of me believes that this is exactly how songs are born, just as some people who are not writers believe that we are entirely dependent on the appearance of a muse.

And, thankfully, the song proper isn't anticlimactic: 'You Had Time' is perhaps the gentlest and most generous-spirited break-up song I know. (And just as the intro is a talentless fan's dream of musical creativity, this generous-spiritedness is a liberal heterosexual's idea of how nice gay women are to each other, even when their relationships fail. While straight men are inwardly plotting revenge while feigning indifference, and straight women are cutting the crotches out of expensive trousers, gay women are hugging and crying and pledging eternal friendship. This is actually offensive nonsense, of course – unhappily, the only intelligent right-on response is to recognize that gays are as violent, unpleasant, pious, judgemental and unreflective as everyone else – but 'You Had Time' is so sweet-tempered that it inspires this sort of embarrassing stereotyping.) What gives 'You Had Time' some of its power is that, whereas most break-up songs are definitively heartsick, this is a song about indecision and stasis. The narrator has just returned from a tour of some kind; both her fingers and her voice are sore, so we must presume that she is a guitarist and singer (you must forgive us, Ani, if we temporarily confuse fiction and autobiography). It becomes apparent that, while away, the narrator is supposed to have sorted out what she wants to do about her relationship, and so the title of the song, it becomes clear, is her lover's predictable and legitimate retort to the age-old plea. Anyway, she's had all this time, and she still hasn't made up her mind . . . Except, the song manages to imply, she has, really: she knows it's over. In one lovely, and very sad, couplet, the narrator says, simply: 'You are a china shop and I am a bull / You are very good food and I am full' . . . See what I mean about generous-spiritedness? How many of us wouldn't have felt better about being dumped if someone said that to us? But the song ends dreamily, with nothing resolved, at least externally, and I doubt that DiFranco will ever write another song quite as piercingly pretty, or as moving.

Mann's song is more straightforwardly about work, and is, I would guess from its detail, unmediated auto-biography, an anecdotal scrap which has been worked and enriched until it contains more resonance than it had any right to. Mann and her band straggle together to play a gig in New York, a gig that none of them seems to have any expectations for; but then 'something strange occurs': the band might not be going anywhere, yet clearly some kind of musical epiphany takes place that night. It's not a happy song, however – Mann chooses to regard the epiphany as ironic (this is our finest hour?) rather than redemptive, and 'I've Had It' becomes a song about the triumph of bitter music-biz experience over hope.

I listen to 'I've Had It' a lot, and there are occasions when I find the tinge of self-pity in the lyric immensely comforting. (Self-pity is an ignoble emotion, but we all feel it, and the orthodox critical line that it represents some kind of artistic flaw is dubious, a form of emotional correctness.) Even so, there's something a little troubling about the song's breathtaking melodic strength. Here's the thing: which came first, the tune or the words? Because if it was the tune, then that makes you wonder why Mann thought music that sublime was best served by her travails in music. Wasn't there a break-up that meant this much to her, or a parent, or a childhood memory? (Her song 'Ghost World', incidentally, contains a verse indicative of what a fine writer she is: 'Everyone I know is acting weird or way too cool / They hang out by the pool / So I just read a lot and ride my bike around the school'. These few words do the job of perhaps as many as 700 recently published semi-autobiographical but deeply sensitive first novels.) And if the words came first, then are we to presume that it is only her career that can produce this level of musical inspiration? Either way it bothers me a little, and makes me doubt whether my love for the song is really to be trusted. This frequently happens in pop music, of course – all sorts of people knock up a neat tune and then can't furnish it with anything but a few tatty second-hand lines about eagles flying and love dying – but one is struck here by what seems like Mann's inability to tame and control her melodic gift. It is, perhaps, the curse of the trade. 'All art constantly aspires towards the condition of music,' Walter Pater said, in one of the only lines of criticism that has ever meant anything to me (if I could write music, I'd never have bothered with books); music is such a pure form of self-expression, and lyrics, because they consist of words, are so impure, and songwriters, even great ones like Mann, find that, even though they can produce both, words will always let you down. One half of her art is aspiring towards the condition of the other half, and that must be weird, to feel so divinely inspired and so fallibly human, all at the same time. Maybe it's only songwriters who have ever had any inkling of what Jesus felt on a bad day.

But what is appropriate subject matter for a song? There are many ways in which songs differ from books, but both songwriters and novelists are looking for material that will somehow mean something beyond itself, something that contains echoes and ironies and texture and complication, something both timely and timeless, and, in the case of pop music, something that will sustain over several hundred plays and, possibly, a couple of margarine advertisements. Sometimes songs seem to survive the going-over they are given by fans and radio stations almost despite themselves, more by luck than judgement. The Clash probably didn't think that 'Complete Control', an attack on their record label for releasing a single without their approval, would make any sense to people a couple of decades later ('They said release "Remote Control"' is surely one of the less promising first lines of a song) but it still has something to say about naivety and cynicism and artistic impotence. Even 'Nelson Mandela' doesn't sound daft, despite the great man's release; it celebrates a life – a great life, an important life, a life well-lived – and therefore easily and joyously transcends the focus of its protest. Nils Lofgren's 'Keith Don't Go', on the other hand, is a song which pleads with The Rolling Stones' guitarist not to go to Toronto in 1977, because he would have been arrested on a drugs rap; it's not a cause that one wanted to devote an awful lot of energy to, even back then (not least because Keith could just, like, not go), and it's not a song that has revealed hidden depths in the intervening years. The great Australian comedian Norman Gunston used to sing Liza Minnelli's 'I'm Liza with a Z' and then profess himself mystified that more people didn't cover it – perhaps Nils is just as bemused that 'Keith Don't Go' hasn't earned him the publishing royalties he'd anticipated.

In the end, it's the songs about love that endure the best. Songs about work are good. Also songs about rivers, or parents, or roads. Good songs about children are surprisingly rare (yes, it's hard to write about the feelings one has for one's child without nauseating people, but somehow songwriters manage to knock out perfectly decent, sometimes even breathtaking, songs about the airhead model they met in the toilet of a club without the same effect); songs about pets are best avoided. Songs about drugs – especially songs that purport to be about girls but are 'really' about drugs – don't have the same appeal when you are no longer at school and there's no one you can explain the hidden meaning to. And jokes never really stand the test of airtime. (I have always felt slightly ambivalent about Randy Newman's work, brilliant though much of it is. How many times do you want to listen to a song satirizing bigotry, or the partiality of American congressional politics? Listening to Randy Newman over and over again is like reading *The Grapes of Wrath* twice a year: however much you care about the plight of America's migrant workers in the 1930s, there is surely only a certain amount of your soul and mental energy you can devote to them.) But the truly great songs, the ones that age and golden-oldies radio stations cannot wither, are about our romantic feelings. And this is not because songwriters have anything to add to the subject; it's just that romance, with its dips and turns and glooms and highs, its swoops and swoons and blues, is a natural metaphor for music itself. Songs that are about complicated things – Canadian court orders, say, or the homosexual age of consent – draw attention to the inherent artificiality of the medium: Why is this guy singing? Why doesn't he write a newspaper article, or talk to a phone-in show? And how does a mandolin solo illustrate or clarify the plight of Eskimos anyway? But because it is the convention to write about affairs of the heart, the language seems to lose its awkwardness, to become transparent, and you can see straight through the words to the music. Lyrics about love become, in other words, like another musical instrument, and love songs become, somehow, pure song. Maybe this is what gives 'You Had Time' the edge: our break-ups, in the end, have more melody to them than our work does.

Born for Me
Paul Westerberg

12

Actually, that's a serious question: how does a mandolin solo illustrate or clarify the plight of Eskimos anyway? In fact, how does any sort of solo illustrate any sort of plight, whether it be the plight of Eskimos, or the plight of a young man whose girlfriend is seeing his best mate behind his back? Why are words suddenly suspended while the guitarist or the sax player or the violinist steps forward and does his thing?

Those of us who were born in the late fifties and fell in love with rock music during the early seventies have a complicated relationship with the solo. I can remember seeing Grand Funk Railroad play in Hyde Park, and trying, with what in retrospect strikes me as a heartbreaking earnestness, to enjoy, appreciate or understand the twenty-minute drum solo; a couple of years later, older and wiser and in a late-teenage, pre-punk, anti-bombast frame of mind, I nipped out of Led Zeppelin's show at Earl's Court during John Paul Jones's interminable keyboard extravaganza, went to a local pub for a game of pool and a pint, and came back just in time to catch the end of Jimmy Page's bit with the violin bow, thus missing 'Moby Dick' (The One with the Drums) completely. I have no regrets. (Not only do I have no regrets, but also, now I come to think about it, that night taught me one of life's most useful lessons, one of the only pieces of advice I have to offer to younger generations: YOU'RE ALLOWED TO WALK OUT! I still remember the feeling of giddy liberation I had when we walked into that pub; and had I not left the Zeppelin show then, who knows whether I would ever have realized that it was possible? Oh, I knew that people walked out because they were shocked. But I didn't know that it was permissible if you were simply a little bored. Since that night I have tasted that sweet relief hundreds of times: I've walked out of films, gigs, and – of course – the theatre. If you sit next to me during the first act of a play and my fidgeting is annoying you, don't worry – I won't be back after the interval. And let me tell you, there's nothing like the taste of pasta and a glass of wine at nine-thirty if you thought you weren't going to be eating until eleven. It is not overstating the case to say that John Paul Jones and his keyboards turned my whole cultural life around.)

Nobody does the extended-solo thing any more – or at least, no one I'm interested in seeing live – so all fears of The Solo have long vanished. (And in any case, we're talking about songs made in a recording studio here, not live shows, so the solos are almost always contained, and always involve a lead instrument, rather than bass or drums.) In fact, since the members of Grand Funk Railroad went their separate ways (although, like everybody else, they have almost certainly since reunited), I have learned to love solos; and, though of course it's possible to find a great song which doesn't have any kind of instrumental break, I would argue that a great song containing a great instrumental break is by definition superior to a great song without one.

There are two kinds of great solo. The first, and more common, type is the one where a brilliant (or momentarily inspired) musician steps forward and fills the allotted number of bars imaginatively – even thrillingly, if you're lucky – but not necessarily appropriately. At the end of Steely Dan's 'Kid Charlemagne', for example, there's a guitar solo of such extraordinary and dextrous exuberance that you end up wondering where it came from, and quite what it has to do with the dry ironies of the song's lyrics; 'Kid Charlemagne' is a typically clever, mordant look at the death of the sixties, but the solo that closes it is the sound of pure, untethered joy; the guitar jumps up on the song's shoulders and then just launches itself toward the clouds, and as the song fades you can tell that it's going to reach them, too. But what the sound of pure joy has to do with 'Kid Charlemagne' and the death of the sixties remains unclear, and in the silence between that track and the next, it's the guitar you're left with, like a single, wonderful flavour that has completely and regrettably overpowered a delicate recipe. Joy is never an unwelcome guest, but some songs are happier to see it than others: Springsteen's guitar solo in 'Thundercrack' (from *Tracks*) comes tumbling ecstatically out of a deliberately discordant screech and, though Springsteen's not the cleverest guitarist in the world (and the song isn't really a song at all, simply a tumultuous way to finish a stage show), he can do that kind of *West Side Story* street-punk energized ecstasy standing on his head, and it always makes me happy to hear it.

But my favourite solos are the ones that somehow show that the soloist has felt the song, words, music and all, felt the song and understood its very being, so that the solo becomes not only an imaginative reinterpretation of it, but also a contribution to and articulation of its meaning and its essence, like a piece of brilliant practical criticism. And sure, this is what solos are supposed to do, but most of them are at best an imaginative reinterpretation of the melody line; very few of them give the impression that they want to engage with the songwriter's soul. David Lindley did this spectacularly on the first few Jackson Browne albums; Clapton did it repeatedly on *Layla*, when he was apparently strung out on heroin and exalted by grief – a blow for those of us who don't want to buy into either of these myths about art. His solo on 'Nobody Knows You When You're Down & Out', a deeply felt, simply played break that seems to pour unstoppably from a deep wound in the centre of the song itself – not the guitarist, but the song – is my favourite white blues-rock moment. Clarence Clemons isn't my favourite soloist – we've heard the same solo too many times – but if I were Bruce I would have wept at what Clemons produced for 'Lovers In The Cold' (a *Born To Run* out-take that you can find on the Net), because I would have felt well and truly understood, and every single swoop and squall is an articulation of devotion to the spirit of the song and of its creator. And the delirious violin solo in the middle of Mary Margaret O'Hara's extraordinary 'Body's In Trouble' hiccups and swoons as if it's on the verge of the kind of fainting fit that young nineteenth-century English women were supposed to have experienced in Florence: you don't get too many attacks of aesthetic ecstasy on your average pop-folk album, but this one nearly overwhelms the song.

The thing I love about these solos is that they can crop up in unexpected places, and they needn't even be parti-cularly well played. Paul Westerberg, everyone's favourite coulda-beena-contender, is no pianist, but his solo on 'Born for Me' is just lovely – maybe because he's the singer-songwriter, and knows what his song feels like to him, and therefore what it should feel like to us. 'Born for Me' is a ragged ballad, with a Waitsian lonely losers' lyric and an affectingly heartsick tune; the solo is basically played with one finger, and initially at least consists of three notes, but it sounds great to me – not in a punky, do-it-yourself way (although frankly you could, once you've heard it), but in a strangely, intensely musical way. A better pianist would have wrecked the moment, filled in the gaps, failed to recognize how the tune has exerted a spell over the right listener; somebody with little talent and absolutely no ear would simply have chosen the wrong three notes. Just as you know intuitively when the simplest and crudest brush-strokes have been made by a proper artist, I can never listen to the solo without thinking that it's played by a born musician – not a virtuoso, not even someone who could make a living as a pianist in a cocktail lounge, just a man who thinks and feels and loves and speaks in music.

13

Frankie Teardrop
Suicide

Ain't That Enough
Teenage Fanclub

14

Suicide's 'Frankie Teardrop' is ten and a half minutes of genuinely terrifying industrial noise, a sort of aural equivalent of *Eraserhead*. Like David Lynch's film, it conveys a chilling, bleak, monochrome dystopia, full of blood-curdling shrieks and clangs, although I seem to remember that the movie offered the odd moment of respite, an occasional touch of bizarre and malformed hope, whereas 'Frankie Teardrop' offers none at all. Here's a cheerful, bowdlerized version of the story: Frankie works two jobs, but even then he can't make ends meet, so one night, in despair, he goes back home, murders his wife and children, shoots himself and ends up in Hell. I would, as you might suspect, be lying if I told you that the ten minutes flew by.

If you haven't heard it and you still wish to, set an evening aside, make sure you're not alone in the room (experiencing the song through headphones, incidentally, will almost certainly result in hospitalization) and take the following day off work. Teenage Fanclub's 'Ain't That Enough', on the other hand, is a three-minute blast of Byrdsian pop, packed with sunshine and hooks and harmonies and good will. I like the Teenage Fanclub song better.

Well, of course I would. It's more likeable. It's got a tune and everything, and on the whole I prefer songs with tunes. 'Frankie Teardrop' is in all sorts of ways an extraordinary piece of work, but I have no use for it now; I listened to it once upon a time, when I was in my twenties and my life was different, but I probably haven't played it for a good fifteen years, and I doubt whether I'll ever play it again. (I didn't even listen to it in order to write this, and didn't feel that I needed to. Believe me, the memory has remained vivid.) I don't want to be terrified by art any more.

It's a strange critical phenomenon that only works of art that are 'edgy', or 'scary', or 'dangerous', are regarded as in any way noteworthy. In my newspaper today, there is an interview with the filmmaker Todd Solondz, whose film *Happiness* was about paedophilia and provided, it says here, 'a lacerating insight into the hypocrisy of the

American middle classes' – an insight I missed, I'm afraid, when I saw the film. There's an interview with a band called British Sea Power, who say that 'there's so much more you can do than just write songs and sing them' and stare psychotically into the camera as they are being photographed. There's a piece about the Jack the Ripper film *From Hell*, which is headlined 'Danger: menace at work'. And a rapper called Bubba Sparxxx is taken to task by a journalist because 'talking about your rural roots isn't exactly edgy, is it?' (Well, no. But that, it seems to me, is a flaw inherent in most conversational topics, unless you are heroically single-minded about it, and wax lyrical about the Nazis or terrorist atrocities every time you go out to dinner. Talking is, by and large, one of the safer things one can do.)

There are, I suspect, two reasons why so much critical interest is excited by edginess or danger. The first is that critics have to read a lot of books, or see a lot of films, or listen to a lot of music, most of which is bland and indistin-guishable, and so anyone who makes a record which features a chainsaw, or a film that runs backwards for twelve hours, is immediately and perhaps understandably praised – in most cases, as weary readers quickly learn if they attempt to share the enthusiasms of their newspaper's

arts pages, overpraised. The second is that reviewing –
especially music reviewing – is, for the most part, a young
person's game, and young people tend not to have had a
great deal of life experience. Not only have they not lived
very much (which is why they tend to get very excited
about anyone with a whiff of hard-drug use about them –
hard-drug use is frequently misinterpreted by rock critics
as a valuable life experience), but they do possibly the safest
job there is to do. Indeed, as most of them get their CDs
sent to them through the post, CDs they then listen to on
their home stereo before filing their reviews via email –
they do not even run the risk of being knocked down by a
bus. Who wouldn't, in these circumstances, get wildly over-
stimulated by an artist who is expressly trying to liven them
up a bit?

Me, I need no convincing that life is scary. I'm forty-four,
and it has got quite scary enough already – I don't need
anyone trying to jolt me out of my complacency. Friends
have started to die of incurable diseases, leaving loved ones,
in some cases young children, behind. My son has been
diagnosed with a severe disability, and I don't know what
the future holds for him. And, of course, at any moment
there is the possibility that some lunatic will fly a plane into
my house, or a nuclear power plant, or attempt to sprinkle

something into our water supply or our Underground trains that will turn us all black as our kidneys shrivel up in our bodies. So let me find complacency and safety where I can, and please forgive me if I don't want to hear 'Frankie Teardrop' right now.

'All these years later and Suicide still feels like a shot in the head,' an enthusiastic reviewer remarked when their first album was re-released; a couple of decades ago, that would have been enough to make me want to buy it. ('A shot in the head! Wow! Even The Clash only felt like a kick!') Now, however, I have come to the conclusion that I don't want to be shot in the head, and so I will avoid any work of art that sets out to re-create that particular experience for me. It's a peculiarly modern phenomenon, this obsession with danger. And, in the end, it's impossible not to conclude that it has been born out of peacetime and prosperity and over-education. Would the same critic have told someone coming back from the Somme that a piece of music 'feels like a shot in the head', one wonders. And if he did, would he really have expected the chap to go charging off to his local music emporium?

It is important that we are occasionally, perhaps even frequently, depressed by books, challenged by films, shocked by paintings, maybe even disturbed by music. But do they have to do all these things all the time? Can't we let them console, uplift, inspire, move, cheer? Please? Just every now and then, when we've had a really shitty day? I need somewhere to run to, now more than ever, and songs like 'Ain't That Enough' is where I run. 'We are all Frankies', Suicide concluded at the end of their *magnum opus*, but they didn't mean it, really, unless they were dafter than they let on. (In what sense have we killed our families and then turned the gun on ourselves, even metaphorically?) And if we were all Frankies, what would we rather listen to? Blood-curdling re-creations of our miserable and unbearable existence, or something that offered a brief but precious temporary respite? That's the real con of shock-art: it makes out that it's democratic, but it's actually only for those who can afford it. And some of us, as we get older, simply find that we don't have that much courage to spare any more. Good luck to you if you have, because it means that you have managed to avoid more or less everything that life has to throw at you, but don't try to make me feel morally or intellectually inferior.

First I Look
At The Purse
the J. Geils Band

15

I fell in love with the USA when I was very young, seven or eight. There was an American kid at my school, and not only did he have toys the likes of which we had never seen (he could make his own toy soldiers, for God's sake, and he could just about hit Saturn with his plastic rocket-launcher), but also he could swivel his eyeballs the wrong way round by pressing hard on his eyelids. Now, the USA sometimes gets a mixed press here in Britain, and there are plenty of people who would find these twin triggers darkly significant: well of course, they'd say, if you're going to glamorize freaks and fetishize weapons, then America is bound to exert a fascination, but for me, there was nothing sinister about either my friend's toys or his talents. It was all about superior American technology (the eyeballs) and superior American entertainment values (the rocket-launcher), and I was left with the indelible impression that just about everything of any interest was better on the other side of the Atlantic.

I didn't visit the US until the mid-seventies, when my father and his family moved to Wilton, Connecticut. I was sixteen, and I lived in a country which, looking back on it now, seemed to be striving for the ambience and amenities of communist Poland rather than those of New York. A series of strikes had resulted in a series of power cuts, which meant that evenings were frequently spent eating sandwiches and reading by candlelight. We had three television channels and no TV during the day anyway, apart from the occasional educational programme about mathematics or the life cycle of the salmon. Our food was famously awful (even our junk food was bad junk food), and you couldn't find anywhere that stayed open much later than eleven p.m. Shops were closed on Sundays. American movies took between six months and a year to crawl to British cinemas, and we had no real film industry of our own. We were working a three-day week. The war had been over for thirty years, but there seemed no real reason why we weren't spending the night sleeping in Tube stations anyway – at least it would have given us something to look forward to.

And in the middle of all this, I got on a plane and flew to New York. That first trip, I wanted to do very little apart from watch daytime TV and go to the shops, and my apparent indolence drove my father crazy: he wanted to take me places and show me things, but he had lived abroad for some years, and was, I think, unaware that his native country had become quite so cheerless; the last time he had lived in England, it was swinging, in the immortal words of Roger Miller, like a pendulum do, but the pendulum had now come to an abrupt and sorry stop. I suspect that any sixteen-year-old English kid who visited the States for the first time during the mid-seventies spent their entire trip watching daytime reruns of *Green Acres* and eating exotic breakfast cereals; to venture any further would have resulted in instant death from over-stimulation. No one, of course, will ever die from over-stimulation in Connecticut. And yet most inhabitants of that sedate state would be surprised to learn just how many thrills it had to offer an English teenager back then. I'm not talking about the coastline or the trees, which were charming but not dissimilar to home; I'm talking about Sam Goody's and Kmart, both of which I visited almost daily, and both of which offered unimagined and inexhaustible delights.

My first novel, *High Fidelity*, was about a guy whose devotion to rock 'n' roll has, in various ways, blighted and retarded his life, and it is probably fair to say that a lot of very important research for that book (in other words, a lot of blighting and retarding) was done during that first trip, twenty years before I started writing it. I didn't know so much about popular music back then, but I had certainly exhausted the potential of my home-town record store. I had never seen a good three-quarters of the records in my dad's local Sam Goody's, however, and I came out with armfuls of improbably priced soul and blues albums. (The things that Sam Goody valued at $1.99 were worth an awful lot more to me.)

It wasn't just the record stores, of course. I was taken to houses which contained bumper pool tables in the basement – we didn't have bumper pool at home. I was taken to McDonald's, and we didn't have that either. Nor did we have ice, on our ponds or in our drinks, or good pizzas, or eight-track stereos in our cars, or swimming pools in our back gardens, or pastrami, or sandwiches three inches thick, or shopping malls, or multiplex cinemas, or La-Z-Boys, or hot dogs in our sports stadia. And, yes, I know it was the comfortable, middle-class Connecticut suburbs I had fallen for, and that millions of Americans were poor, and endured environments that were ugly and brutal and hard. But I was a middle-class kid, and I lived in the comfortable English suburbs, and they weren't anything like this. It wasn't as if we had any diverting equivalents, either. We didn't have great pasta and great ice-cream, like the Italians, or great beaches and great soccer, like the Spanish; in the 1970s we were trying to live the American life, but without any of the things that make an American life bearable. What we did have was history, and this, apparently, was enough to make us feel superior.

Well, it didn't do the trick for me. I would cheerfully have
swapped England's entire heritage – Stonehenge, Stratford,
Wordsworth, Buckingham Palace, the lot – for the ability to
watch quiz shows in the morning.

My father's friends had a son called Danny, who was
older than me, maybe twenty or twenty-one, and he had
long hair and a moustache; he looked exactly like Billy
Crudup in *Almost Famous*. Danny loved his music, and the
music he was listening to when I went round to his house
for the first time was the live J. Geils Band album, *Full
House*. I'd never heard of them, and I'd never heard anything like them; in those days, before they had a big pop hit
with 'Centerfold', they played white-boy R&B, like The
Stones in 1965, but much louder and much faster, with a
berserk irreverence and an occasionally terrifying intens-
ity. On the live album, Peter Wolf, the lead singer, shouted
out funny, weird or incomprehensible things in between
songs: 'On the licking stick, Mr Magic Dick!' 'This used to
be called "Take Out Your False Teeth Mama . . . I Want To
Sssssuck On Your Gums"' and something that sounds like
'areyougonnagetitmoodoogetitgoomoogetitmoodoogoo-
moodoomoogetitalldowngetitallrightgetitoutofsightand-
getitdownbaby?' The first thing you hear on the record is a
solid slab of crowd noise, whistles and cheers and screams,

and then a shouted and very un-English introduction from an MC: 'Are you ready to get down? I said, are you ready for some rock and roll? Let's hear it for the J. Geils Band!'

And then, straight away (no tuning up or mumbled 'How you doing's), the band tears into 'First I Look At The Purse', an old Smokey Robinson song that he wrote for a Motown group called The Contours, and even old Smokey Robinson songs seemed to come from a parallel universe. The ones I knew were sweet and sad, like 'Tracks Of My Tears' or 'Tears Of A Clown', but this one was straightforwardly nasty – the message of the lyric was that any man who cared about how a woman looked or what she was like was a fool. 'I don't care if she waddles like a duck or talks with a lisp / I still think I'm a good lover if the dollar bills are crisp'. At the end of the song the band plays faster and faster and Wolf sings faster and faster until the whole thing blurs into a mess of noise, and then the audience roars as if greeting the winning goal in the World Cup Final. (And this was the opening number, the loosener, the warm-up – by the end of side two things start to get really rowdy.) To me back then, this, not Tamla Motown, was The Sound of Young America – loud, baffling, exotic, cool, wild. It comes from the same place as Kramer in *Seinfeld*, and 'Surfin' Bird', and 'Papa-Oom-Mow-Mow', and James Brown being wrapped in a cape and led off stage before bounding back to the microphone, and Muhammad Ali's boasts, and the insane celebrations when a contestant won a lawnmower on *The Price Is Right*. In our quiz shows, people smiled when they won. Not always, though.

I eventually saw the J. Geils Band for myself, some six years later, but I saw them in Hammersmith rather than Detroit, where *Full House* was recorded, so the atmosphere was respectful rather than insane, and, though they were soon to become much more successful, they were past their peak. And I saw them on 12 May 1979, the night that Mrs Thatcher was elected Prime Minister for the first time. We drove back to college just as old Britain was turning into modern Britain – ironically, a dour and tacky version of America, with the McDonald's and the shopping malls, but without the volume or the delirium or the showmanship. 'I'm so bored with the USA', The Clash were singing on stage every night around that time, and, though we all sang along with them, it wasn't true, not really. We were only bored with our obsession, and that's a different thing entirely.

7. # Smoke

(B. Folds, A. Goodman)

Leaf by leaf page by page
Throw this book away
All the sadness all the rage
Throw this book away
Rip out the binding tear the
glue
All of the grief we never even
knew
We had it all along

Now its Smoke
The things we've written in it
Never really happened
All of the people come and
gone
Never really lived
All the people come have gone

No one to forgive smoke
We will never write a new one
There will not be a new one

Another one, another one
Heres an evening dark with
shame
Throw it on the fire
Heres the time I took the
blame
Throw it on the fire
Heres the time we didnt
speak
It seemed for years and years
Heres a secret
No one will ever know the
reasons for the tears

They are smoke

Where do all the secrets live
They travel in the air
You can smell them when
they burn
They travel
Those who say the past is
not dead
Stop and smell the smoke
You keep on saying the past
is not dead
Come and smell the smoke
You keep saying the past is
not even past
You keep saying
We are, Smoke

Smoke
Ben Folds Five

16

We're sitting in my back garden on a hot summer night, eating barbecued chicken and listening to Todd Rundgren, when a friend suddenly explodes into a rant about pop music. His argument, as far as I could follow it, went as follows: it's crap because the words are crap, pathetic adolescent poetry rather than lyrics, and so if it's all crap then you might as well listen to music that performs a function and has no pretensions whatsoever . . . Which is why he only bothers with house music. House music doesn't bother with words very much, and has an express goal, namely making you dance when you're off your face.

This, it seems to me, is like saying that because most restaurants are very bad, one should play the percentage game, forget about trying to find the good ones, and eat at McDonald's every meal. There is no doubt, though, that lyrics are the literate pop fan's Achilles heel. We have all lived through the shrivelling moment when a parent walks into a room and repeats, with sardonic disbelief, a couplet picked up from the stereo or the TV. 'What does that mean, then?' my mother asked me during *Top of the Pops*. '"Get it on / Bang a gong"? How long did it take him to think of that, do you reckon?' And the correct answer – 'Two seconds, and it doesn't matter' – is always beyond you, so you just tell her to shut up, while inside you're hating Marc

Bolan for making you like him even though he sings about getting it on and banging gongs. (I suspect that this humiliation continues, and that it makes no difference whether the parent doing the humiliating was brought up on a diet of T. Rex, or Spandau Ballet, or Sham 69, and therefore should really avoid the literary high ground altogether. My mother, after all, belonged to a generation that danced – danced and *smooched* – to 'How Much Is That Doggie In The Window?' and if she felt able to be snooty about 'Get It On', then surely snootiness is a weapon available to all. Rubbishing our children's tastes is one of the few pleasures remaining to us as we become old, redundant and culturally marginalized.) I do not, despite (or possibly because of) my day job, pay that much attention to the lyrics of my favourite songs. 'Call Me' by Aretha Franklin, pretty much the entire lyric of which runs 'I love you / So call me the moment you get there', is the last word in any argument about whether greatness in a song is attainable without lyrical ambition or complexity. (The last word, that is, unless someone wishes to point out that a great song must by definition offer a little more than a line or two of what sounds like a particularly uninspired telephone conversation. Well OK, but 'Call Me' still gets further down the road towards something wonderful than is easily explicable.)

Half-heard phrases don't worry me, and I am happy to let anything pass which does not actually make me blush.

The more forgiving one is of one's favourite artist's literary pretensions or inadequacies, however, the easier it is to forget that songwriting is an art distinct from poetry. You don't have to be Bob Dylan, and you don't have to be whoever writes the songs for Celine Dion (in other words, you don't have to use the words and phrases 'dreams', 'hero', 'survive', or 'inside my/yourself', because life isn't an ad for a new type of Ford); you can, if you're brave, have a go at being Cole Porter, and aim for texture, detail, wit and truth. Ben Folds is, I think, a proper songwriter, although he doesn't seem to get much credit for it, possibly because rock critics are less impressed by sophisticated simplicity than by sub-Dylanesque obfuscation: his words wouldn't look so good written down, but he has range (on his second album there are songs about apathy masquerading as cool, an unwelcome guest, and the ugly triumphalism of a bullied nerd made good), an amused eye for lovestruck detail ('Words fail when she speaks / Her mix tape's a masterpiece', he sings on the ecstatic 'Kate') and he makes jokes – but not in the choruses, crucially, because he knows that the best way to wreck a joke is to repeat it seven times in three minutes.

'Smoke' is one of the cleverest, wisest songs about the slow death of a relationship that I know. Lots of people have assailed the thorny romantic topic of starting all over again (for example, off the top of my head, 'Starting All Over Again', by Mel & Tim), and the conclusion they usually come to is that it's going to be tough, but both practicable and desirable; the heartbreaking thing about Folds's song is that it manages simultaneously to convey both the narrator's desperation and the impossibility of a happy outcome. He doesn't know about the latter, though – only Folds the songwriter, who has the benefit of both music and a vantage point, can see that the relationship is doomed.

In 'Smoke', the central conceit is that the relationship is a book, and so its unhappy recent history, the narrator wants to believe, can be destroyed by burning it page by page, until 'all the things we've written in it never really happened'. 'Here's an evening dark with shame', he sings. 'Throw it on the fire!' the backing vocalists tell him. 'Here's the time I took the blame. (Throw it on the fire!) Here's the time we didn't speak, it seemed, for years and years . . .' Wiping the slate clean is the fantasy of anyone who has ever got into a mess with a partner, and the metaphor is witty enough and rich enough to seduce us into thinking just for a moment that in this case it might be possible, but the music here, a mournful waltz, tells a different story. It doesn't sound as if the narrator's lover is terribly convinced, either: 'You keep saying the past's not dead', he tells her, 'Well, stop and smell the smoke'. But the smoke, of course, contains precisely the opposite meaning: it's everywhere, choking them. 'You keep saying . . . we're smoke', he concludes sadly, and we can tell that he's beginning to believe it, finally; the smell of smoke, it turns out, does not symbolize hope but its opposite.

'Smoke' is, I think, lyrically perfect, clever and sad and neat, in a way that my friend would not credit; it's also one of the very few songs that is thoughtful about the process of love, rather than the object or the subject. And it was a constant companion during the end (the long, drawn-out end) of my marriage, and it made sense then, and it still makes sense now. You can't ask much more of a song than that.

It's possible that this sort of craft goes unnoticed because 'Smoke' is 'just' a song, in the way that 'Yesterday' or 'Something' weren't 'just' songs. The young men who wrote them were also, unwittingly or not, in the process of changing the world (or – to attempt to cover all the arguments in one clumsy parenthesis – in the process of being given credit for changing the world, unwittingly or not). This inevitably means that an awful lot of attention was focused on their talent – which, after all, was ostensibly the only world-changing tool at their disposal. If you're singers, and you're changing the world, then people are bound to look pretty closely at what you're singing – because how else are you doing it? As a consequence, some very good, very pretty, very sharply written, brilliantly produced and undeniably memorable songs have been credited with an almost supernatural power. It's what happens when people are deified. The eighteenth-century British scholar Edmond Malone calculated that Shakespeare 'borrowed' two-thirds – 4,144 out of 6,033 lines – from other sources for *Henry VI*, Parts I, II and III. And, though *Henry VI* is a minor play, the point is that this stuff was out there, in the world, and Shakespeare inhaled it. What he exhaled was mostly genius, of course, but it was not genius that came out of the blue; it had a context.

The Beatles had a context, too, but they seem to have inhaled that along with everything else: they have hoovered up and become the sixties, and everything that happened in that extraordinary decade somehow belongs to them now. Their songs have therefore become imbued with all sorts of magic that doesn't properly belong to them, and we can't see the songs as songs any more.

Ben Folds has not changed the world, and nor has he changed popular music. (Indeed, at the time of writing, he may well be struggling to earn his living from popular music, although I hope not.) He is writing songs at a time when nobody equates music with social change; he has no context to hoover up, and he is working in a medium (loosely, pop/rock) that at the time of writing – and, let's face it, at the time of reading, unless you're reading this in 1970 – is widely regarded as washed-up, exhausted, finished. So his songs are just songs. They represent nothing, and nor are they a part of anything else, and they must fight for attention in an industry and a critical climate that is only interested in cultural significance.

This is what has to change, if pop music is to survive. Literature seems to have just about maintained a toe-hold in our culture because we're prepared to accept that books can be *sui generis*: Zadie Smith's *White Teeth*, for example, represents nothing but itself. It isn't at the forefront of a new, young, hip, multicultural, etc., literary revolution, and it belongs very firmly to a familiar narrative tradition. But that doesn't make it any less of an achievement, or any less interesting; and it certainly hasn't made it unpopular, either with critics or with readers. If it had been a record, however, we'd probably have ignored it; the general view would have been that we've heard all that great writing and ambitious narrative stuff before, thanks very much, and we're waiting for something new to come along.

There is an argument which says that pop music, like the novel, has found its ideal form, and in the case of pop music it's the three- or four-minute verse/chorus/verse song. And, if this is the case, then we must learn the critical language which allows us to sort out the good from the bad, the banal from the clever, the fresh from the stale; if we simply sit around waiting for the next punk movement to come along, then we will be telling our best songwriters that what they do is worthless, and they will become marginalized. The next Lennon and McCartney are probably already with us; it's just that they won't turn out to be bigger than Jesus. They'll merely be turning out songs as good as 'Norwegian Wood' and 'Hey Jude', and I can live with that.

A Minor Incident
Badly Drawn Boy

17

'You must be excited about the film coming out,' a friendly and well-meaning acquaintance remarked at the end of 2001, a few months before the movie version of *About A Boy* was released. (Those weren't her actual words. Her actual words were, 'You must be excited about *About A Boy* coming out.' I changed them because, prose stylist that I am, I wanted to avoid that double 'about'. I'm sick of it. My advice to young writers: never begin a title with a preposition, because you will find that it is impossible to utter or to write any sentence pertaining to your creation without sounding as if you have an especially pitiable stutter. 'He wanted to talk to me about *About A Boy*.' 'What about *About A Boy*?' 'The thing about *About A Boy* . . .' 'Are you excited about *About A Boy*?' And so on. I wonder if Steinbeck and his publishers got sick of it? 'What do you think of *Of Mice and Men*?' 'I've just finished the first half of *Of Mice and Men*.' 'What's the publication date of *Of Mice and Men*?' . . . Still, it seemed like a good idea at the time.)

I smiled politely, but the supposition mystified me. Why on earth would I get excited? There had been interesting, sometimes even enjoyable bits along the way – selling the rights to the book for an unfeasibly large sum of money, for example, meeting the people responsible for the film version, seeing the end product, which I liked a lot. I'd be very suspicious, however, of any writer who was actually excited by any of this process, which can be on occasion distasteful (*About A Boy* ate up a director and got spat out by another film company even before it was made) and stupefyingly prolonged; indeed, the time before, during and after a film's release is positively unpleasant. You get reviewed all over again; you discover that half your friends never read the book in the first place; the bits of the film people like the most turn out to be nothing to do with you.

But the first time I heard the soundtrack to the film really was exciting, in the proper, tingly sense of the word. Seeing one's words converted into Hollywood cash is

gratifying in all sorts of ways, but it really cannot compare
to the experience of hearing them converted into music:
for someone who has to write books because he cannot
write songs, the idea that a book might somehow produce
a song is embarrassingly thrilling.

Like a lot of people, I spent a large chunk of 2000
listening to and loving Badly Drawn Boy's *The Hour of
the Bewilderbeast* album. It's one of the very few English
records of recent years I've had any time for; it's thoughtful, quirky without being inept (despite my earlier presumption that the name of the artist was somehow indicative of
the ramshackle nature of the music, a presumption that
stopped me from listening to him for a while), it's melodic,
it borrows lightly and judiciously from all sorts of folky,
rocky things I like (Damon Gough is an early-Springsteen
devotee), it doesn't show off, it is un-English in the sense
that it wouldn't be much use to Ibizan clubbers or boozed-
up football hooligans, it has soul. It also sounds cinematic,
with its little snatches of orchestration (it begins with a
brass-band instrumental that would not have sounded out
of place in a gentle sixties comedy) and its range of moods.
It seemed to me that Damon could write a wonderful film
score, and I would have suggested him for *About A Boy* had
I not known that writers have less chance of influencing

film adaptations of their books than they do of changing the weather. And then, the first time we met, Chris and Paul Weitz, the co-directors, told me that they had already asked Damon to provide all the music for the film. This struck me as being troublingly neat – could it really be possible that the music in my head was the same as the music in theirs? – but anyway, here I am, in my office, listening to a whole lot of new Badly Drawn Boy songs and music cues that very few people in the world have heard yet, and feeling lucky.

I began writing *About A Boy* in 1996, the year my son Danny was finally diagnosed as autistic. There were lots of things to think (or panic, or despair, or lose sleep) about, and money was only one of them, but I suddenly went from feeling reasonably wealthy – I was in my fourth year of earning a decent whack from writing, and for the first time in my life I had some savings – to financially vulnerable: I was going to have to find enough to make sure that my son was secure, not just for the duration of my life, but for the duration of his, and that extra thirty or forty years was hard to contemplate, in more or less any direction. And then, no sooner had these worries begun to take hold and chafe a little bit than this Hollywood money arrived. Until the movie was made, this was the only connection I had forged between the book and Danny. The character of

Marcus was nothing to do with him (Marcus is twelve, and brightly voluble, if odd; Danny was three, and five years later is still unable to speak), and I don't think that Danny would recognize the parenting that Marcus experiences. It's possible that, if I had been childless, I would have been attracted to a different kind of story, but that's the only way that *About A Boy* is about Danny.

'A Minor Incident', a sweet, heartfelt, acoustic strummer with a wheezy Dylanesque harmonica solo, refers directly to a major incident in the book and the movie: Marcus comes home from a day out to discover his mother, Fiona, lying comatose on the sofa after an attempt to kill herself, her vomit on the floor beside her. The song is her suicide note to her son. I wrote one for her too, but it wasn't in the form of a song lyric, and Damon's words capture Fiona's dippy, depressive insouciance perfectly. But here's the thing: once I'd listened to 'A Minor Incident' a couple of times, it started to make me think of Danny in ways that I hadn't done when I was writing the book. 'You always were the one to make us stand out in a crowd / Though every once in a while your head was in a cloud / There's nothing you could never do to ever let me down', sings Damon as Fiona, and the lines brought me up short. Autistic children are by their nature the dreamiest of kids, and Danny's ways of making us stand out in a crowd can include attempts to steal strangers' crisps and to get undressed on the top of a number 19 bus. But that peculiar negative in the last line ... How did Badly Drawn Boy know that it's the things that Danny will never do (talk, read, play football, all sorts of stuff) that make those who love him feel the most fiercely proud and protective of him? And, suddenly, five years on, I find a mournful undertow of identification in the lyric to the song, because the money from the sale of the film rights has forced me to contemplate my own mortality; like Fiona, I'm thinking of a time when I won't be around for Danny – for different reasons, but the end result is the same.

So there we go. That's where the excitement lies: in the magical coincidences and transferences of creativity. I write a book that isn't about my kid, and then someone writes a beautiful song based on an episode in my book that turns out to mean something much more personal to me than my book ever did. And I won't say that this sort of thing is worth more than all the Hollywood money in the world, because I'm a pragmatist, and that Hollywood money has given Danny a trust fund which will hopefully see him through those terrifying thirty or forty years. But it's worth an awful lot, something money can't buy, and it makes me want to keep writing and collaborating, in the hope that something I write will strike this kind of dazzling, serendipitous spark off someone again.

Glorybound 18
The Bible

The Bible are a now-defunct English band who you probably won't remember. They got good reviews, and they had a near hit in '86 or '87 with a song called 'Graceland', and towards the end of the eighties they were able to fill medium-sized venues in the UK, but they split after a couple of albums, to the sorrow of thousands, although possibly not hundreds of thousands; the absence of a more frenzied and universal grief tells its own tale. There are countless bands like The Bible, bands with talent, loyal and discriminating fans and a couple of good albums in them, but the wrong sort of record label, or manager, or haircut, or trousers, or simply the wrong sort of luck. My record collection is full of albums by groups who didn't quite

manage the long haul – Friends Again, and Hot!House, and
The Keys, and Danny Wilson, and Hurrah! (avoid those
exclamation marks, kids, if you want a long career in music
– The Bible had one once, and dropped it, but it was too
late) – and all of them, it seems to me, could have gone on
to fame and fortune if ... Oh, never mind. Pop snobs
always think that the bands they love have been treated
unfairly, that their failure is evidence of a tasteless, ignor-
ant and tone-deaf world, but the truth is that invariably
these bands are too quiet, too anonymous, too ugly, too
smart and they've spent too much time listening to Chris
Bell or The Replacements or Bill Evans instead of dressing
up, taking drugs, trying out make-up and picking up
fourteen-year-olds; I may prize the songwriting craft of
Paddy McAloon over the vulgarity of Eminem, but it
would be stupid to pretend that I don't know why Eminem
is the bigger star.

Anyway. I learned to love The Bible because a couple of
the band members were friends, or at least, friends of
friends – Boo Hewerdine, The Bible's lead singer and songwriter, worked in The Beat Goes On, a record store in
Cambridge, with my friend Derek, so Boo and I were on
nodding terms, when Boo could be bothered to nod. (Later
I found out that it wasn't rock-star arrogance that made

him look through me when we passed each other in the street, but chronic short-sightedness. His myopia still serves him well – on stage he looks as though he's lost in his music, when in fact he stares straight ahead because he doesn't know where else to look, and he can't wear his glasses because they get steamed up.) I presumed – well, you do, don't you? – that he and his band would be embarrassingly talentless, and that once I'd heard his first record I wouldn't know how to keep the pity out of my nods; in fact his first record was intimidatingly good, and I was duly intimidated. I started going to see the band play a lot, in their various incarnations (before they were The Bible! or The Bible they were The Great Divide, and Georgia Peach) and with varying degrees of elbow room: there were about seven of us watching when they were a support act at the Marquee in 1984; four years later I couldn't get in when they played the Town & Country Club, which holds a couple of thousand. (I did know Boo well enough to get on the guest list, honest. It's just that I'd forgotten to ask him, and I didn't think there'd be a problem, and . . . Oh, believe what you want.)

It is only when you know and love a band that you become the kind of music critic that every magazine and newspaper should employ. I have been doing some writing about pop for *The New Yorker* over the last couple of years, a gig that necessitates having hundreds of CDs you don't want thrust through your letter box every morning. (I suspect that the record companies somehow end up guessing your tastes and cunningly omitting the CDs you might want from their mail-outs, thus obliging you to buy them anyway.) My usual response to these unwanted CDs is as follows: a) I look at the cover. If it has a Parental Advisory sticker, and the artist is called something like Thuggy Breakskull, or PusShit, I don't play it. Nor do I bother if the artist in question is pretty, or has big hair, or is snarling, or has blood coming out of his or her nose, or looks like he or she has appeared in a teen soap, or looks very old, or looks very young, or simply vaguely clueless (a complex judgement, this last one, and possibly not one I can describe coherently – something to do with the eyebrows, I think, although occasionally there is a helpful tattoo, or smile, or sneer, or item of headwear), or records for a label that I don't like. Sometimes – although admittedly not often – I turn the CD over, to check song titles, song lengths, occasionally the name of a producer, hoping something will lead me to conclude that this album is Not For Me – that it's for teens, or squares, or ravers, or headbangers, or Conservatives, or anarchists, or just about anyone other than a 44-year-old who lives in North London and likes Nelly Furtado and Bruce Springsteen. If I still haven't managed to form an antagonistic prejudice, then b) I look at the press release. If it uses as a comparison any of the approximately 300,000 names whose music I don't have time for (and it usually does, because my 300,000 names have been very carefully chosen), well, I don't play it then, either. So very, very few albums make it as far as step c), which is where I actually put the fucking thing in the CD player and listen to it. 'Listening', however, in this context, means waiting for the first chord change in the first track, at which point I can breathe a huge sigh of relief and dismiss the whole thing out of hand as a joke, a talent-free zone, a cacophonous mess created by know-nothings. It's a pretty impregnable system.

I do concede that it's not a fair system, however, and if you or your record company have, in the last couple of years, sent me an album that you were hoping I might review in *The New Yorker*, I can only apologize, and suggest that next time you don't wear a stupid hat in the photo shoot for the cover art. (And if you have a nosebleed, then please wait until it stops and you've cleaned yourself up.) If, however, you ever worked in a record store with one of my friends, you can expect entirely different treatment. I will listen to every song you ever record. The ones I don't like very much on first hearing, I will play again, on the assumption that I must have missed something the first time around. And if I still don't like something, I will not allow this rogue composition, this one bad apple, to contaminate my enjoyment of the next, almost certainly great, track.

'Glorybound', a pretty, mid-tempo shuffle which begins, promisingly (promisingly, note, and NOT, in this case, derivatively, as would have been the case with a song sung by someone who used to work in some other record shop that I've never been in), with the same two-note bass riff as 'Rikki Don't Lose That Number' (which in turn starts with the same two-note bass riff as Horace Silver's 'Song For My Father', so you could argue that The Bible are respectfully honouring a glorious musical tradition), and which contains a gorgeous, slinky guitar solo by my other friend in the band, Neill MacColl, was a B-side, but that, of course, didn't stop me from finding it and playing it and playing it until it became a part of me, a permanent deposit in my tune bank. And that's what music needs: this kind of devotion, this assumption that the artists know what they're doing and that, if you give them the time and the requisite confidence, they will deliver something you will end up cherishing. Who knows how many great songs I've missed (and 'Glorybound' is a great song, that's the whole point – this is not about how I'm making a silk purse out of the family sow's ear, but about how I usually end up doing the opposite), songs written and performed by people who are your friends but not, unfortunately, mine?

Caravan

Van Morrison

19

The magnificent version of 'Caravan' on *It's Too Late to Stop Now* (Van Morrison's most enjoyable album, unarguably, so don't even think about arguing) sounds to me like it could be played over the closing credits of the best film you've ever seen; and if something sounds like that to you, then surely by extension it means that it could also be played at your own funeral. I don't think this is over-dramatizing the importance of one's own life. Not all films have to be like *Lawrence of Arabia* or *Apocalypse Now*, and you'd have to have been pretty unlucky, at least in our part of the world (and if you walked into a bookshop and bought this book, you live in the part I'm talking about), not to have experienced a few moments of joy or pure hope or clenched-fist triumph or simple contentment amongst all the drudgery and heartbreak and pain. To me, 'Caravan' recognizes and synthesizes all of it, and the fact that what it produces from the whole extraordinary mess is something that sounds cheerful doesn't mean that the song is trite.

'Caravan' isn't a song about life or death, as far as I can tell: it's a song about merry gypsies and campfires and turning up your radio and stuff. But in its long, vamped passage right before the climax, when the sax weaves gently in and out of the cute, witty, neo-chamber strings, while the piano sprinkles bluesy high notes over the top, Morrison's band seems to isolate a moment somewhere between life and its aftermath, a big, baroque entrance hall of a place where you can stop and think about everything that has gone before. (Gosh. A sudden panic: can you hear any of that, those of you who already own the album or who are interested enough in this description to check it out? Possibly not. But – panic over – this book isn't predicated on you and me sharing the ability to hear exactly the same things; in other words, it isn't music criticism. All I'm hoping here is that you have equivalents, that you spend a lot of time listening to music and seeing faces in its fire.) And, though it won't be me doing the thinking, as far as we know, is it arrogant to expect a little reflection from friends and family? It's my funeral, after all. And they don't have to think only about me; they can think about all sorts of things, as long as they're worthy of the occasion and the music, and don't involve foodstuffs, emails, footwear, etc.

The only thing that worries me about having 'Caravan' played at my funeral is that string section. Will people think I'm making some concession to classical music when they hear it? Will they say to themselves, 'What a shame he lost the courage of his convictions right at the end there, just like everybody else'? I wouldn't want them to think that. Unless something unimaginable happens to me over the next couple of decades, I will have gone through an entire life listening more or less only to popular music in one or other of its forms. (I have a few classical CDs, and sometimes I play them, too; but I never respond to Mozart or Haydn as music, merely as something that makes the room smell temporarily different, like a scented candle, and I don't like treating art in that way, with disrespect.) And I'm unrepentant, too. 'I'd see him banged up for having anything to do with the inanity that is pop, full stop,' said a famously sour writer and newspaper columnist recently, while attempting to defend a well-known music-business mogul who had just been imprisoned, but you've heard this stuff before.

I have no idea whether his use of the word 'pop' is the same as mine, whether he thinks that all of it, Dylan and Marvin Gaye and Neil Young, is inane. I suspect he does. It's not a complaint I've ever understood, because music, like colour, or a cloud, is neither intelligent nor unintelligent – it just is. The chord, the simplest building-block for even the tritest, silliest chart song, is a beautiful, perfect, mysterious thing, and when an ill-read, uneducated, uncultured, emotionally illiterate boor puts a couple of them together, he has every chance of creating something wonderful and powerful. I don't want to read inane books, but books are built from words, our only instruments of thought; all I ask of music is that it sounds good. Despite its crudity and simplicity, 'Twist and Shout' sounds good – in fact, any attempt to sophisticate it would make it sound much worse – and I fundamentally, profoundly disagree with anyone who equates musical complication and intelligence with superiority. It doesn't work like that, which is maybe why these people despise pop music, because it's one of the very few things that doesn't. (They often hate sports, too.) I don't dislike classical music because of its cultivation – I'm not an inverted snob. I dislike it (or at least, I'm unaffected by it) because it sounds churchy, and because, to my ears at least, it can't deal with the smaller feelings that constitute a day and a week and a life, and because there are no backing vocals or basslines or guitar solos, and because a lot of people who profess to like it actually don't really like any music (or any culture) at all, and because I grew up listening to something else, and because it does not possess the ability to make me feel, and because I don't need my music to sound any 'better' than it does already – a great, farting, squelching, quick-witted sax solo does the job for me. So 'Caravan' will be played at my funeral.

The problem with the extended passage that I mentioned earlier, the bit that I hope will make the mourners think and reflect is that . . . Well, OK, here's the thing: it's the bit where Van Morrison introduces the band. 'Terry Adams on cello . . . Nancy Ellis on viola . . . Bill Elwin on trumpet . . . David Hayes on bass . . .' Is that too weird? Can people really file out of my funeral listening to a list of names of people they (and I) don't know? I've started to think of this passage as a sort of metaphorical dramatis personae now: granted, I don't know David Hayes or Nancy Ellis, but, you know . . . I probably knew someone like them. That's the best I can come up with, and it'll have to do, because I'm not changing my mind, so there.

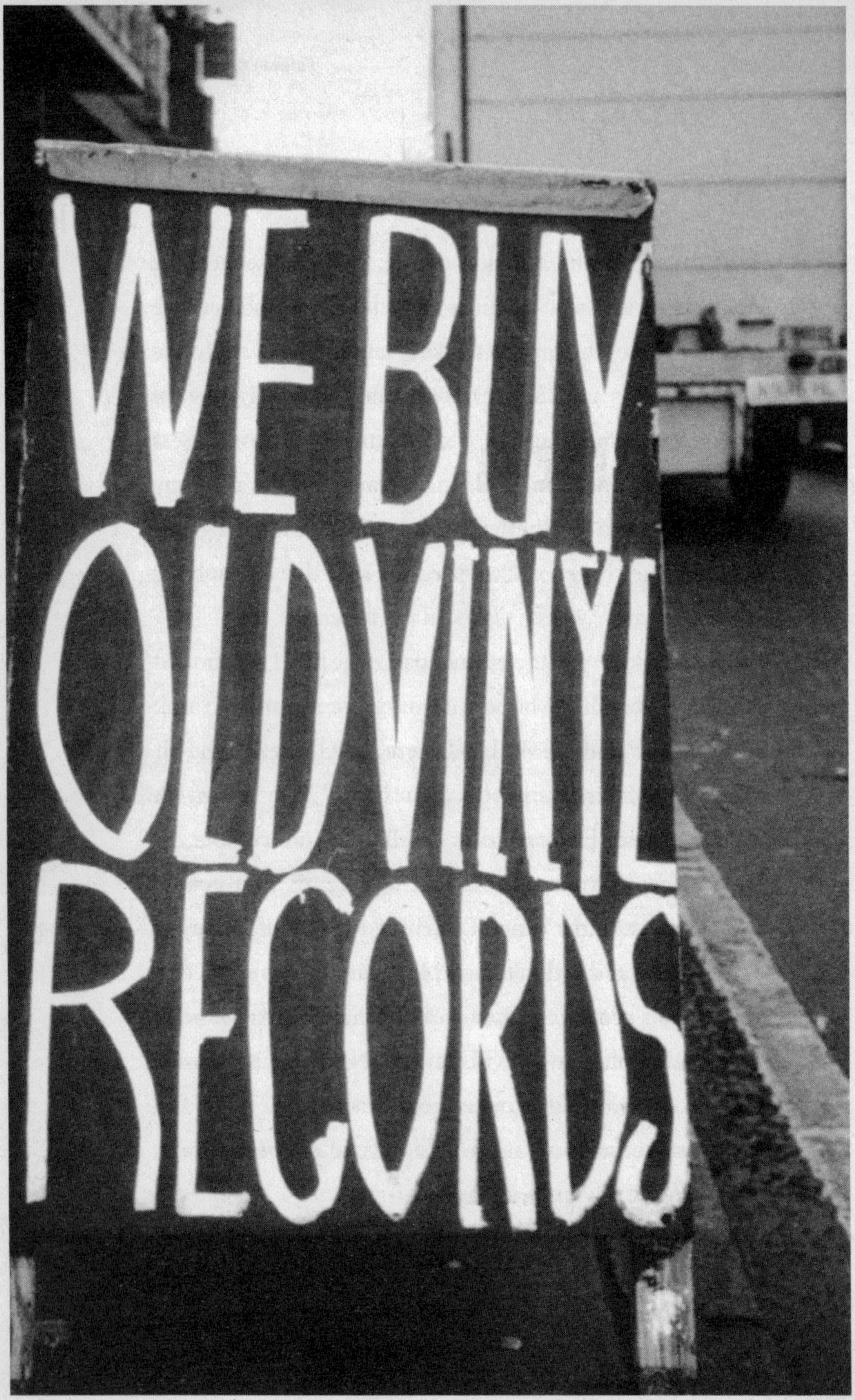
WE BUY
OLD VINYL
RECORDS

So I'll Run 20
Butch Hancock and Marce LaCouture

Some time in the late eighties, I went to see Butch Hancock, the Texan singer-songwriter, play in a large and draughty local pub. I distinctly remember feeling underwhelmed by the prospect on the way there. It was a cold, wet London winter night, and I wasn't in the mood, and the pub was notoriously grim and there have been times when I've found solo acoustic shows hard work, a little too much meat and potatoes and not enough dessert. But Butch Hancock is a legendary figure in country-folk music, and he'd come a long way, and he certainly wasn't in Finsbury Park very often . . . It seemed churlish not to go.

But Butch wasn't playing on his own. He was accompanied that night by another singer, a woman called Marce

LaCouture, and the moment the show started my mood was lifted. They sounded terrific together, this pair, and it seemed like a small miracle that two throats and one acoustic guitar could transform the draughty (and frankly three-quarters empty) pub into a place where nice things could happen.

After a while they took a break. Marce stayed around to sell cassettes from the side of the stage, and I bought one off her, having first ascertained that it contained 'So I'll Run', the song I'd liked the most in their first set. (It turned out that 'So I'll Run' was just about the only song they played that wasn't theirs – it was written by someone called Al Strehill, and I still don't know who that is – so my enthusiasm for it was probably slightly tactless.)

Anyway, that was it. I had a nice time, nicer than I'd expected, and then I went home. But for some reason, when I was writing *High Fidelity*, the evening came back to me, and I made Rob, my narrator, go to a shitty pub to see a singer-songwriter called Marie LaSalle. He likes the music, not least because it lifts, or at least alters, his mood, and he buys a cassette off her in the interval, and develops a crush on her. Later, she visits him in his record store, and they end up sleeping together. I am sure that Ms LaCouture would confirm – with hurtful alacrity – that we didn't sleep together. And she'd also confirm, probably with similar alacrity, that she didn't play a cover of Peter Frampton's 'Baby I Love Your Way', and she certainly didn't visit my record store, because I've never had one. And even though she seemed very nice, I didn't develop a crush on her; I don't even think I had a passing fantasy about dating a musician and being thanked in the sleeve notes of her CDs, as Rob does while he's watching Marie perform. And yet I know that my Marie character somehow derived from her, which is why she has a similar name and the same initials. I suspect that it wasn't Marce LaCouture I was writing about, but the song she sang. I had retained memories of the evening because of the alchemy she wrought in turning a wet night and a crappy PA system into a few moments of magic, and I was effectively trying to do the same. Like her, I was stuck with unpromising ingredients (a morose narrator and his moronic friends, a dismal pub), and, like her, I was trying to entertain people despite the idiotic restrictions I had imposed on myself. Recently I have been attacked in newspapers by two 'fabulist' writers, as far as I can make out for the ordinariness of the worlds I portray. To which the most obvious reply is that it's all very well writing about elves and dragons and goddesses rising out of the ground and the rest of it – who couldn't do that and make it colourful? (Readable, of course, is another matter . . .) But writing about pubs and struggling singer-songwriters – well, that's hard work. Nothing happens. Nothing happens, and yet, somehow, I have to persuade you that something is happening somewhere in the hearts and minds of my characters, even though they're just standing there drinking beer and making jokes about Peter Frampton. Genius is an overused word, but . . . No, OK, I won't push it. The point is that I gave my character the same initial letters as the singer I'd seen because I was hoping that something might rub off, that somehow this would make it easier for my readers to understand how my narrator's mood might be transformed because, in similar physical circumstances, mine had been. In other words, it was pure superstition.

I have done this before and since, presumably to similarly little purpose. The first thing I ever wrote, a TV play that I never sold, I wanted to sound like the piano part on the intro to Aretha Franklin's 'I Say a Little Prayer'; maybe the reason I never sold the play is that the piano part is less than thirty seconds long, which isn't really enough to sustain a whole play. *About A Boy*, my second novel, was intended in some way to resemble 'E-Bow the Letter' by R.E.M. How? I don't know how. I just know that there was a tone in the song that I wanted to replicate in the book, something simultaneously mysterious and wry and reflective. Generous readers might give me the wry part of it, anyway. And, though I have never managed to pull any of this off to my own satisfaction, though I have never read any of my books or scripts back and said to myself, 'Yep, that's it, that's exactly what I wanted it to sound like', I know that without the pieces of music the writing would have been so much harder. So, thank you, Marce and Butch. Without you, Rob would never have got to sleep with a singer-songwriter, and he would definitely have been the unhappier for it.

21
Puff the Magic Dragon
Gregory Isaacs

I can remember the first time my son Danny was exposed to music. He'd just come back with his mum from the hospital where he was born, and I played Shara Nelson's solo CD, which I was playing a lot that autumn, and he suddenly became very still and watchful. It's impossible not to sentimentalize the first few days of a child's life, but I'd have been willing to bet then that music was going to be important to my son, in some way or another – not a stupid bet, considering how important music is to his mother and me. Maybe he'd turn out to be merely a fan; maybe he'd end up playing an instrument. Didn't – doesn't – matter to me either way, just so long as he felt it somewhere in him.

It was a very happy time of my life. Danny was home and safe, after a difficult birth which had endangered him and nearly killed his mother; meanwhile she and I had, we felt, put a long period of difficulty behind us shortly before his conception, and his emergence into the world was confirmation that these troubles would not be returning. Things didn't stay good for very much longer, though. Danny's development was a constant cause for concern (it would be some time before he was diagnosed as autistic), and, perhaps unsurprisingly, given the stress of those first few years, the Elastoplasts fell off his parents' patched-up relationship, and the wounds underneath had gone gangrenous.

But through it all, Danny continued to feel the music – he feels it so much, in fact, that he invented his own word for it, which is no mean feat when your inability to communicate defines your world. One of the many fascinating things about his condition (and yes, there's fascination there too, just as there is laughter and pleasure and excitement, mixed in with the heartbreak and worry) is that, though he has very little language, he has managed to find words for things he fears he might not be given unless he asks for them. In other words, there are some things so desirable that they can burst through the blanket of silence that smothers him, and music ('goggo', as he calls it) ranks right up there, along with crisps, and swimming, and biscuits, which is pretty much where I'd put it, too.

Danny's relationship with music is an intense one. He has to listen before going to sleep at night; he sometimes wanders round with a portable cassette player, volume turned up as high as it will go, and occasionally he retreats to his bedroom, like a teenager, in order to listen with a concentration not permitted him elsewhere. I find it almost overwhelmingly moving, watching him when he does that – my little speechless boy, his head lowered on to the speaker, all the better to absorb every note (and – who knows? – maybe every word) of every song.

And he seems to be developing tastes, too. A couple of weeks ago, in the car, he listened quite happily not to his usual nursery rhymes but to *Tapestry*; but when the CD-changer switched to Louis Armstrong's *Hot Fives and Sevens*, an outraged cry came from the back seat: 'Goggo! Goggo!' Louis Armstrong, the man who single-handedly created one of the most important musical idioms of the twentieth century, did not, apparently, create music. So we moved on to Nick Lowe instead, and he was happy again. This was good news. Any sentence pertaining to Danny that incorporates the words 'developing' and 'tastes' is good news, because he tends to get stuck, to focus wholeheartedly on the tastes he already has (for salt and vinegar crisps, and Postman Pat videos, and peanut-butter sandwiches), rather than developing new ones: there was a brief open window of opportunity, somewhere between his first and third birthdays, through which he was prepared to admit new experiences and flavours and interests, but this window was shut suddenly, with a bang and with no warning, and any addition to his repertoire in the last five years has been a cause for rejoicing and baffled conversation – 'He watched twenty minutes of *Toy Story*!' 'He ate half of a cracker!' 'He did a poo at school!' This is the sort of thing that passes for radical innovation in Danny's life; you may think of yourself as a creature of habit, but he's gone way beyond creature. He's the Beast, the Tyrannosaurus rex, of habit.

So I've got high hopes for music. I'm trying to switch him from cassettes (which he tends to mangle) to CDs, and to move him away from nursery rhymes; I reckon he could cope with, I don't know, *Rumours*, or *Rubber Soul*, or *Catch A Fire*, as long as I could get him to listen to the first few bars – usually, all foreign cultural matter (videos he has never seen, music he has never heard) is expelled via the eject button immediately. I've had some modest success recently with a CD called *Reggae for Kids*, which begins with Gregory Isaacs singing 'Puff the Magic Dragon', and this modest success comes hot on the heels of another modest success, the introduction of a world music thing that, though he never requests or attempts to play himself, is tolerated and perhaps even quietly appreciated, and I've found a couple of other collections that he might get into . . . Who knows? Maybe soon he'll be listening to Gregory Isaacs singing 'Night Nurse'. And then we could maybe go to a gig, and he'll be motivated enough to want to learn which CDs come out of which case . . . When you have a child with a disability, you learn to let go of the ambitions you once had for him very quickly (and you learn too that many of those ambitions were worthless anyway, beside the point, precious, silly, indulgent, intimidatingly restrictive), but they get replaced by others, and ambitions involving music (the listening thereto, rather than some daft *Shine*-style fantasy involving the Royal Albert Hall, an extraordinary talent and a disbelieving, tearful audience) seem both harmless and achievable.

But to begin with, listening to 'Night Nurse' would be enough. If it's true that music does, as I've attempted to argue elsewhere, serve as a form of self-expression even to those of us who can express ourselves tolerably well in speech or in writing, how much more vital is it going to be for him, when he has so few other outlets? That's why I love the relationship with music he has already, because it's how I know he has something in him that he wants others to articulate. In fact, thinking about it now, it's why I love the relationship that anyone has with music: because there's something in us that is beyond the reach of words, something that eludes and defies our best attempts to spit it out. It's the best part of us, probably, the richest and strangest part, and Danny's got it too, of course he has; you could argue that he's simply dispensed with all the earthbound, rubbishy bits.

22

Reasons To Be Cheerful, Part 3
Ian Dury & the Blockheads

The Calvary Cross
Richard and Linda Thompson

23

You could, if you were perverse, argue that you'll never hear England by listening to English pop music. The Beatles and The Stones were, in their formative years, American cover bands who sang with American accents; the Sex Pistols were The Stooges with bad teeth and a canny manager, and Bowie was an art-school version of Jackson Browne until he saw the New York Dolls. But you'll never hear England by listening to Elgar or Vaughan Williams, either: too much has happened since then. Where's the lager-fuelled violence? Where's the lip, or the self-deprecation, or the lethargy, or the irreverence? Where are the jokes? Where's the curry? You may not want to think about any of that when you lie back and think of England, but it's all undeniably there, and if you're English, the odds are that you'll eat a curry more often than you see an ascending lark.

You couldn't really find anything more American-sounding than the music Ian Dury's band the Blockheads play on 'Reasons To Be Cheerful': chicken-scratch James Brown guitar, a sax solo which quotes from the theme to *A Summer Place* . . . except, right there, in that odd combination of late-fifties American kitsch and early-seventies American funk (and 'Reasons To Be Cheerful' is funky enough to bring on a patriotic, we-can-do-it-too glow), there is something uniquely English: Dury's generation was not afraid of the past, nor of popular culture outside the rock and blues tradition. (Compare The Beatles or The Kinks to just about any American band of the same era, and you can only conclude that our bands liked their parents more.) 'Reasons To Be Cheerful' is, as its title implies, a list, and in the way the list consists of a great many things that are not English, it is as curiously representational of a certain kind of post-war Englishness as the music. Stephen Biko, for example, the black activist who was murdered by the South African authorities, was an integral part of our liberal-left political landscape of the early eighties – it was an English singer, Peter Gabriel, who wrote a song about him. And the trombonist Rico is Jamaican, but our 1970s obsession with reggae wasn't shared on the other side of the Atlantic, and Rico was a reason not only to be cheerful but also why The Specials sounded so distinctive (and, at the time, so distinctively un-American). I'm not attempting to claim British credit for any of these people or their achievements, merely pointing out that they are meaningful to us, that they are part of what being British has involved in the last few decades.

The more I listen to 'Reasons To Be Cheerful', the more it sounds like the best kind of national anthem, one capable of inspiring pride in those of us who spend too much time feeling embarrassed by our country. In fact, if Tony Blair has any guts, he should explain to the Queen that, because none of us cares about her any more, the old anthem is no longer applicable, and that Dury's tune will henceforth be used at all sporting events and state ceremonies. Just imagine: before each England international, David Beckham sings 'Summer, Buddy Holly, the working folly, Good Golly Miss Molly and goats', while the rest of the team chants 'Why don't you get back into bed?' The boost to national morale would be incalculable. And the beauty of it is that the song could evolve. If we decided as a nation that, say, Jarvis Cocker or Judi Dench or Michael Owen are reasons to be cheerful, then the Poet Laureate would be told to knock up a couplet for insertion. (An added bonus would be that we could dispense with military bands, none of whom possesses the requisite swing, let alone the requisite electric guitars.)

There hasn't been much, certainly since punk, to inspire pride in anyone who doesn't buy the John Major vision of Britain, a vision involving old ladies cycling to evensong and cricket; the re-energizing effects of Tony Blair's election in 1997 are long gone now that he and his government have been exposed as a bunch of hollow, career-preserving hacks. I can't get excited about our foolish, phony gangster films, or most of our leaden, snobby authors, or much of our leaden, philistine pop music (and if you think all pop music is philistine, then compare Lennon's influences – the Goons, Chuck Berry, music hall, Surrealism, loads of things – with Noel Gallagher's, which seem to consist entirely of The Beatles). But Dury's song is a reminder that there is (was?) a different British heritage, something other than Cool Britannia and Merchant Ivory. 'Reasons To Be Cheerful' mentions Health Service glasses (we still have a Health Service), and the Bolshoi Ballet (we never had a Red Scare) and singing along to Smokey (we love, have always loved, our black American music – indeed, we have turned into its curators – and we never thought that Disco Sucked) . . . And when Ian Dury gives thanks, in that art-school Cockney voice, for 'something nice to study', it almost breaks your heart: self-teaching, too, is part of our twentieth-century history (think of the Left Book Club, Penguin's original remit to provide cheap classics to the masses, the Open University) although one suspects that it isn't going to be a big part of our twenty-first. For a piece of funk whimsy, 'Reasons To Be Cheerful' is culturally very precise, if you listen to it closely enough; whether it refers to a vanished golden age, only time will tell.

In Richard Thompson's 'The Calvary Cross', it's possible to hear an older England, the one that Blake and the Brontës write about, the old, scary place, full of dark satanic peasants and howling winds and pigs' bladders and what have you. And though there is a lot of English folk music that can conjure up those dark days, when there were only three terrestrial TV channels and no decent takeaways, Thompson is the only one who does it using an electric guitar – he's swallowed rock 'n' roll whole (he's not averse to the odd Chuck Berry cover, and his version of The Byrds' 'Ballad of Easy Rider' is a wonderful, folk-inflected hybrid of Here and There) and coughed up something that could only have been made in Britain. The first time I saw him and his ex-wife Linda perform, in 1977, they looked like a couple of Hardy characters: the gig was in an austere lecture theatre in Cambridge, and Thompson's gaunt, haunted, old-fashioned face made me think of poor Jude Fawley and his doomed attempts to study at Oxford. Linda, meanwhile, was wearing a smock and a headscarf, sat on a stool (she may have been pregnant) and looked miserable, as though Thompson were trying to sell her, just like Henchard sold his wife in *The Mayor of Casterbridge.* It was all very bleak, and curiously memorable, and though I'm glad I saw them, I never felt for a moment as if I lived, or even wanted to live, in the country that had produced their music. Does that matter? Probably not – I have never wanted to live in Mali, or in Trenchtown, Jamaica, either, but I've got a few good records that have come from those places. It's just a little uncomfortable, though, hearing music of and about your native land that makes your native land sound like the coldest, bleakest place on earth. I want to live where Ian Dury lived; I hope I still do.

Late for the Sky
Jackson Browne

What was I listening to in 1974, when 'Late for the Sky' came out? Not Jackson Browne, for a start. I wasn't really aware of him until 1977, when my musical microclimate was way too ferocious to accommodate delicate Californian flowers; the ubiquity of 'The Pretender' in all the record collections of the girls I met at college confirmed my suspicion that when it came to music, girls didn't Get It. And then, a couple of decades later and going through a marriage break-up, I found that *Blood On the Tracks* and *Tunnel of Love*, having been mined exhaustively during peacetime, didn't have much left in them, and meanwhile, The Clash and the Ramones, the people who, I felt, had wanted me to turn my nose up at 'The Pretender', had long since ceased to be much use to me. (Which is not to say that the college girls had, after all, Got It back then. We were nineteen – we should all have been listening to punk, not listening to songs about marital discord and early mid-life crises, although consid-ering that the boys were listening to punk while studying English literature or law at the University of Cambridge, you could argue that either option involved an element of make-believe that young adults should have grown out of.) So, after taking advice from my friend Lee (q.v.), I returned home with a couple of Jackson Browne albums, and found within minutes that I had made a new friend.

I didn't know any of the great songs on those first three or four albums, apart from 'Doctor My Eyes' and 'Take It Easy'. I'd never heard 'Late for the Sky', or 'These Days', or 'For a Dancer', or 'From Silver Lake', or 'Jamaica, Say You Will'. It was almost like discovering a writer I'd never read – except we discover writers we've never read all the time, and only rarely, as adults, do we stumble across major pop artists with a decent back catalogue: it is usually prejudice rather than ignorance that has prevented us from making their acquaintance, and prejudice is harder to overcome (indeed, much more fun to maintain). And, yes, of course it was prejudice that had stopped me from listening to Jackson Browne. He wasn't a punk. He had a funny pudding-bowl haircut that wasn't very rock 'n' roll. He wrote 'Take It Easy', at a time when I didn't want to take it easy. And though I hadn't heard any of the songs, I knew they were wimpy, navel-gazing, sensitive – American in all the worst ways and none of the best.

And suddenly, there I was, aged forty-plus, lapping it all up, prepared to forgive all sorts of lyrical infelicities and banalities in the sad songs; prepared to forgive, too, all the limp, hapless, thankfully rare attempts to rock out (although I would have been much less forgiving in vinyl days, when I had no access to a remote control and a skip button). I'm prepared to forgive the bad stuff because the best songs are simply beautiful, and beauty is a rare commodity, especially in pop music, so after a while anything which stops you from embracing it comes to seem self-injurious. I can't afford to be a pop snob any more, and if there is a piece of music out there that has the ability to move me, then I want to hear it, no matter who's made it. I used to have a reason not to like Little Feat (too polite, as far as I can recall, and maybe too musically precise) and Neil Young (over-long guitar solos) but no one can nurse those kinds of quirks in taste now. You're either for music or you're against it, and being for it means embracing anyone who's any good.

The pop snob's dismissal of people like poor Jackson would be forgivable if everything we spent our snobbiest years listening to was of comparable worth, but of course most of it was the most terrible (and ephemeral) rubbish. Recently, *Mojo* magazine ran their list of the 100 Greatest Punk Singles, and it would be fair to say that probably eighty of them were and remain simply awful – derivative, childish, tuneless even within the context of punk, nothing I would ever want to hear again. And yet at the time I would have taken Half Man Half Biscuit or The Users over Jackson Browne any day of the week. (What am I talking about? I did take Half Man Half Biscuit over Jackson

Browne, every day of the week.) I didn't hear David Lindley's hymnal, soulful guitar solo in 'Late for the Sky' for a quarter of a century because I was a bigot, as narrow-minded and as dumb as any racist. (And speaking of which: I was old enough to vote, and yet still I made excuses for 'Belsen Was A Gas' by the Sex Pistols, while simultaneously finding myself unable to absolve a man for an iffy haircut and a touch of introspection . . . It was all pretty scary back then, now I come to think about it.) Now, I feel far more belligerent about Jackson Browne than I ever did about the Pistols: 'You don't like "Late for the Sky"? Well, fuck you, because I don't give a shit.'

This may simply mean that I have become old, and so therefore Jackson Browne's sedate music holds more appeal than punk – that all this is a long-winded way of saying that I'm forty-five (today, as I write!), and so I listen to folky singer-songwriters now, not bratty and loud guitar bands . . . kids . . . lower-back pain . . . a nice night in watching *The West Wing* . . . blah blah. And yet I still appreciate, and recognize the value of, noise, as my partner would no doubt unhappily concur. None of my friends likes The Strokes as much as I do (although admittedly this is because they feel they've heard it all before, whereas I like having heard it all before, so this might not be the incontrovertible evidence of hard-rockin' eternal youth I'm looking for); Marah's recent live shows, the volume of which reminded Lee of Ted Nugent at his most terrifying, simply made me realize that I should allow my ears to ring more often. So I don't think that my new-found love for Jackson can be explained away by my advancing years.

He would have been wasted on me at the time, though; I wouldn't have understood. I'm not referring to the lyrics, which, after all, are hardly opaque (my late-seventies singer-songwriter Elvis Costello made me work much harder at my practical criticism); I'm referring to the soul. And that's where being older helps, because just as I was mistrustful of any melody that didn't come wrapped in a heavy-metal riff when I was fourteen, I was at twenty-one unable to distinguish between soft rock that expressed pain, and soft rock that expressed a smug stoner's content with his wife, his dog, and his record-company advance. There are so many bits in Jackson Browne's music that I don't think I could have responded to as a young man, because their delicacy and fragility I would have mistaken for blandness. The fragment of chorus in "The Times You've Come", when he sings, in a climactic harmony, 'Everyone will tell you it's not worth it', the piano intro to 'I Thought I Was a Child', the first few bars of 'Late for the Sky' itself, when Lindley's

guitar, Browne's piano and an organ create a breath-
takingly sombre beauty (and how many record labels
would allow a major artist to kick off an album with that
now?) . . . You have to have lived a little, I think, to be able
to recognize the depth of feeling that has shaped these
moments, and these songs, and if 'Late for the Sky' is
perfect accompaniment to a divorce, it's not just because
its regretful lyrics fit; it's because divorce peels away yet
another layer of skin (who knew we had so many, or that
their removal caused such discomfort?), and thus allows us
to hear things, chords and solos and harmonies and what
have you, properly. I should add that I'd rather not hear
things properly, that part of me wishes that I had all those
extra layers of skin, and I was still in a position to dismiss
the music as Californian piffle. But I'm not, and I'll have
to make the best of it, and to tell you the truth, the
best of it is much, much better than I could possibly have
imagined. And isn't that just like life?

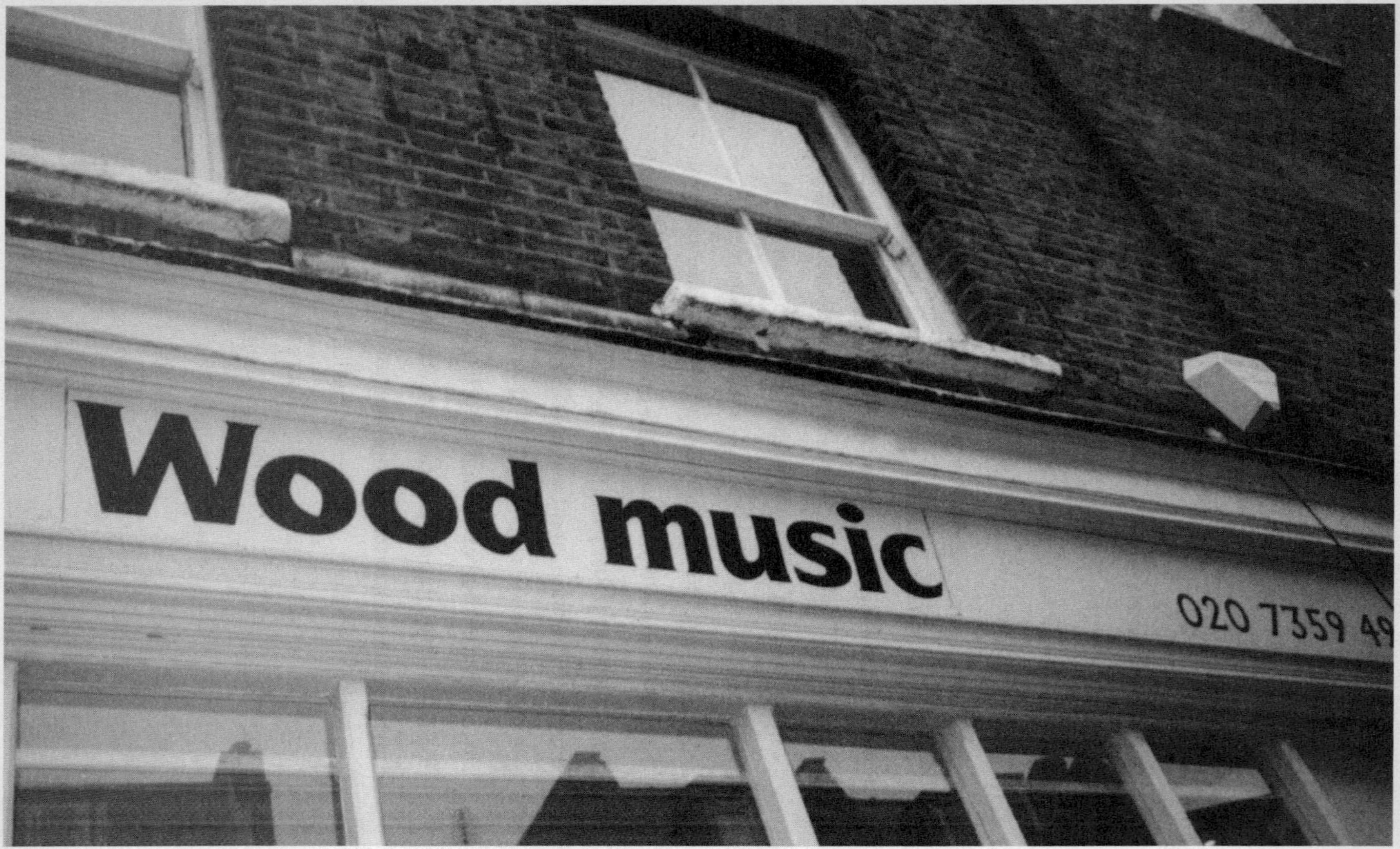
Wood music
020 7359 49

Hey Self Defeater
Mark Mulcahy

25

Some time in 1996, soon after the paperback edition of
High Fidelity was published, I walked into a small music
shop on Upper Street, in Islington, North London – not
very far from where I had placed the fictional small record
shop which the narrator of my novel owned. I'd never been
into this particular shop before – it was relatively new (it
had opened, in fact, round about the time *High Fidelity* was
first published, a coincidence that has led to a great deal of
confusion since) – and in any case, for some reason – the
smartness of the shop, perhaps, or its name, Wood, which
somehow suggested a taste for jazz, or medieval music or
something – I'd always presumed it didn't sell my kind of
stuff. But it did, and I've been using it ever since.

Lee, the proprietor, wasn't there on the day I first visited. He'd gone to Liverpool, to see Bob Dylan, an unambiguous indication that he was serious about his music. Later, when I met him, I found that he was serious about his football, too, just as I am, and that when his two passions clashed, the collision was spectacular and bloody: Dylan was playing Liverpool the night that England was playing Germany in the semi-final of Euro '96, and Lee had got straight off the train to watch the game in a pub round the corner from the concert hall. The game went into extra time, and then there was the agony of the penalty shoot-out . . . He walked out of the pub just as the last Dylan fans were walking out of the gig. He'd travelled 200 miles to watch England play on the TV. This was a man I could do business with.

I have much to thank Lee for. His appearance in my life came at a time when one can find one's commitment starting to eat itself; without him, I can imagine an increasing reliance on reissues and reviews in broadsheet newspapers, which would eventually have led to dissatisfaction with most new music (because I would have been tempted to shell out for a daring new hip-hop album that I'd never play) and therefore, eventually, with music itself. Your old music cannot sustain you through a life, not if you're someone who listens to music every day, at every opportunity.

You need input, because pop music is about freshness, about Nelly Furtado and the maddeningly memorable fourth track on a first album by a band you saw on a late-night TV show. And no, that fourth track is not as good as anything on *Pet Sounds* or *Blonde On Blonde* or *What's Going On*, but when was the last time you played *Pet Sounds*?

I wouldn't have missed out on Lauryn Hill or Radiohead if I had never met Lee (although he's very good at telling me whether or not to believe the hype, and has more than once told me not to bother, to put my credit card away, and you can't ask more of a retailer than that), because nobody misses out on Lauryn Hill or Radiohead; but I would have missed out on people like Mark Mulcahy, whose first album, *Fathering*, I bought on his recommendation, and played repeatedly for months. 'Hey Self Defeater', the first track (and the song that made it on to just about every compilation tape I made that year), manages to convey an earned optimism and compassion through the filters of truth and a sort of conversational sarcasm; it talks to you, and to sarcastic, compassionate people just like you, and me, and because there aren't many of us, apparently (although God knows why, seeing as sarcasm and compassion are two of the qualities that make life on Earth tolerable), it was only ever going to find its audience through word of mouth and recommendations by the like-minded, which is where Lee comes in.

It wouldn't have mattered much in the greater scheme of things, of course, if I had never heard Mark Mulcahy (or Rahsaan Patterson, or D'Angelo, or Belle & Sebastian, or Hazeldine, or Elliott Smith, or Whiskeytown, or Son Volt, or Remy Shand, or Stacey Earle, or Eddie Hinton, or The Jayhawks, or Oh Susanna, all of whom were first encountered at Wood); none of them is, was, or will be the next Marvin or Dylan, or even the next Gram Parsons. But then, like I say, if you're going to stick rigorously to the Greater Scheme diet, then it's *Blonde On Blonde* and *Pet Sounds* – and *Don Quixote* and *Moby-Dick* – for you, breakfast, lunch and dinner. Elliott Smith is my bag of peanuts, and Rahsaan Patterson my Ben & Jerry's; life would be inedible without them.

And all my life I have relied on others to tip me off, enthusiasts effectively and happily serving as Austenesque matchmakers between eligible wallflower music and those who have the capacity and resources to love it. It's people like these who are the difference between a feeble little CD collection that will fit into some stupid designer tower, and a wall of shelves occupying a disproportionate part of your living room.

Update

Lee – like anyone who owns a small music retail outlet – hasn't been doing so well recently. The first half of 2002 has so far failed (despite my clearly foolish optimism, expressed elsewhere in these pages, about the never-ending supply of good new music) to produce just about any half-decent albums; the British music industry's current obsession with boy bands, and girl bands, and boy-and-girl bands, and the winners of TV talent contests, isn't much use to anyone trying to provide music for adults. At the time of writing, there is a danger that Wood might go out of business.

I have sometimes been less than wholehearted in my enthusiasm for independent shops. Oh, of course I will always try to avoid giving my money to chain stores if I can help it; it's just that sometimes, if you're looking for an obscure American import album, or an arcane book of non-fiction, you'll have a much higher strike-rate if you go to the biggest fuck-off branch of Tower or Borders that you can find. This is regrettable, but forgivable, because a lot of small stores can't afford to take a punt on something that will sit ignored on their shelves and in their browser racks for months and months.

But what we will miss, when our entire culture is sold through one big chain-store shopping mall called Border-stones, is the stuff that floats to the surface on a bubble of personal enthusiasm. It's fine if you have some prior knowledge of your obscure American album. But what if you didn't even know that you wanted to hear it? How will you notice it then, among the piles of Jennifer Lopez albums? The most depressing thing about chains is being confronted by the same books and DVDs and albums everywhere you go, the same bestseller lists, the same three-for-two offers. (And yes, before any smart-arse points it out, I too am sick of seeing my books everywhere when I go shopping.) I would like to continue to discover new things; that isn't going to happen anywhere that's floated on the Stock Exchange. Please shop at Wood, or your nearest equivalent, or you'll be sorry.

Wood Music ceased trading in the summer of 2003.

26

Needle in a Haystack
The Velvelettes

One tries hard to avoid exemplifying cliché; looking at the art on your walls and the books and CDs on your shelves, you see only a well-rounded and uncategorizable human who has successfully avoided stereotype all your life. If you are a white male, however – especially a white male aged forty-plus – the chances are that you are sadly and predictably deficient in one particular area: you can't dance for toffee. Indeed, not only can you not dance, but you are also unwilling even to try unless you're drunk or near-drunk, and unless you're surrounded either by complete strangers (especially complete strangers who are older and/or even more disastrously uptight and stiff-limbed than you are) or by people you have known for a minimum of a quarter of a century, who are also drunk or near-drunk. I would love to be able to say, at this point, that I have shattered the mould; that despite my age, gender and nationality (because Englishness, I fear, is hardly helpful in this regard), I hit the dancefloor with all the enthusiasm and lack of self-consciousness of a three-year-old (and a three-year-old girl, at that) and the fluidity of a young Baryshnikov . . . But of course, I can't. The dancefloor is still, to me, the social equivalent of the North Sea during English seaside holidays – something to be treated with the utmost fear and caution, something you walk towards and away from over a period of several hours while battling with your own courage, something you plunge into briefly and uncomfortably while every corpuscle in your blood screams at you to get out before it's too late, something that leaves lots of important parts of you feeling shrivelled.

When I was in my mid-teens, I used to go to a dance every single Saturday night somewhere in my neighbourhood, in order to meet girls, but of course I never actually used to do any dancing. To go to a dance in order to dance would have been like going to a theatre in order to act: the evidence of your own eyes told you that some people did it, but you didn't know any of them. You simply paid to watch them.

Part of the trouble was the music I actually listened to in my mid-teens. You may as well have attempted to eat it as dance to it. Heavy rock was not light on its feet – that was the whole point of it – and though there was great dance music being made at exactly the time when I was attending dances, I wasn't interested in it. In fact, we heavy-rock fans rather despised it for its lack of seriousness. (I would, inevitably, spend much of the next decade trying to buy it all, at three or four times the prices I would have to have paid at the time.) Punk, which obliged one to jump up and down very fast while pushing somebody else over, was hardly designed to make me any more supple or elegant.

But then, in the mid-eighties, I found myself once again attending dances of my own volition, and I wasn't even going in order to pick up girls. I went because I loved it. The club was called The Locomotion, and it took place every Friday night in Kentish Town, in North London; for a while I would feel miserable if I was not able to attend, just as I did when I couldn't see my football team play. The DJ, a woman called Wendy May, played a brilliant mix of funk, Motown, ska, campy pop (Tom Jones's 'It's Not Unusual' was a floor-filler) and, occasionally, house music, which had only just been invented, and had not yet become the ubiquitous pest that has since overrun clubs; everything I heard made me want to dance, and for some reason I was able to. (When I say 'I was able to' I mean, of course, simply that nothing prevented me, rather than that I was suddenly granted the power of eloquent Terpsichorean expression. The Locomotion was a magical kingdom, but it couldn't work miracles.) It's a version of The Locomotion that Rob revives in *High Fidelity*, as those who used to attend know.

Wendy May's taste helped. The Motown songs she played sounded perfect, but they weren't the Motown songs I knew and had tired of. The Velvelettes' razor-sharp 'Needle in a Haystack', for example (which I went straight out and bought – along with George McCrae's 'Been So Long', and

'Groovin' With Mr. Bloe', and loads of other things), I'd never heard before: like all good DJs, May somehow succeeded in making the song hers, something that distinguished and defined her club. It probably helped – as it always helps with me, in any field – that she was so clearly a fan.

But it wasn't just the music. I felt that I understood the people, too – they were all early to mid-thirties, scruffy and relatively impoverished; they didn't and couldn't intimidate me, and very few of them looked as though dancing was something that they were thinking of doing professionally: liking it didn't apparently mean that you had to be brilliant at it. I still had to have a few drinks to take the plunge, but it was only a few: I didn't have to drink until I had grown four legs and had convinced myself (paradoxically) that I could have left a 25-year-old James Brown open-mouthed in admiration. I still liked to watch, too. There was nothing better than to look down from the balcony in the Town & Country Club, listen to great music, and watch several hundred people have the best Friday night you could possibly have in Kentish Town.

And then I stopped going, for reasons that escape me now – probably age had something to do with it, the increasing inability to operate on Saturday morning after a good Friday night – and I went back to being my usual, hopelessly embarrassed, self, as if I had indeed left a magical kingdom behind. Wendy May lives in the country now, apparently, but recently she put on a one-night-only revival at a different venue, right down the end of my street. I didn't go. Well, I would have felt a right idiot, wouldn't I?

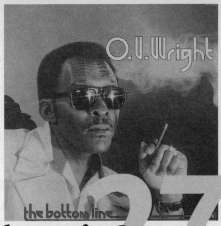

the bottom line

Let's Straighten it Out
O. V. Wright

27

In the early eighties, after punk had died its slow death, I found it hard to care about white rock music very much. Some of my people – Costello, Springsteen – made a decent album every now and again, and a couple of great bands – R.E.M., the Smiths, Dexy's Midnight Runners – emerged to help us forget Those We Had Lost. But mostly, it seemed, the pubs and clubs and record racks seemed to be filled by bands who had absorbed punk's ramshackle amateurism and none of its point, bands who wore long green raincoats and didn't make jokes very often. They were po-faced in ways only the young want to be, and at twenty-four or twenty-five I was just old enough to want to sneer at their earnestness, just as at eight or nine I wanted to go to bed a little later than my sister: those age differentials are important when you're very young.

But black music was for grown-ups; soul songs were about divorces and adultery and lived lives, and it was possible to find big soul artists hitting the peak of their game: Bobby Womack, Anita Baker, Luther Vandross, Prince, Cameo, Marvin Gaye, Teena Marie (who was white, but hung out with Rick James and made albums for Motown) and the producers Jimmy Jam and Terry Lewis all made great records in the first half of the eighties. By contrast, in rock music – as Gramsci said, probably in one of his *Rolling Stone* reviews – the old was dying and the new could not be born, and a variety of morbid symptoms were appearing. And the soul shows were a revelation: a mixed-race crowd having a great time, whooping and dancing (as in, dancing, with feet and bodies and bottoms, as opposed to pogoing or shaking their heads), invariably terrific sound, musicians who could play. You couldn't even argue that white rock bands were serving a different function, because a lot of them, in England at least, had discovered funk. Disastrously, however, they weren't very funky. Why would you want to listen to a twenty-year-old bass player with an apparently arthritic thumb and wearing a kilt attempt an old James Brown bassline, when you could go and hear Cameo play 'She's Strange'?

And now that I had begun to investigate black music, it became clear that there was an enormous amount of back-catalogue to catch up on – so many labels that used the same songwriters and same musicians for their lesser-known acts as they did for their stars, so many albums that contained a hit single but nine other completely unfamiliar tracks. Ann Peebles's recordings for Hi didn't quite reach the peaks of Al Green's best work, but she made pretty good music nevertheless – how could she not? She was produced by Willie Mitchell and backed by the Memphis Horns. And though I knew that Shirley Brown's 'Woman To Woman' was a great 45, I didn't know it was a great 33⅓ too. If you were still determined to listen exclusively to new white rock, then you were almost certainly listening to something that was less than great (and something which, unlike Peebles's 'I'm Gonna Tear Your Playhouse Down', would make you cringe today).

But for me, at that time, one of the best things about it was its maturity. One evening a housemate brought a new boyfriend home; he was an older guy, a writer who wore a trilby, pretty intimidating in all sorts of ways; we got talking about music, as you do, and of course he was a jazz fan, and didn't listen to my kind of stuff: it was 'too teenybop', as if The Osmonds and The Clash were inter-changeable – and, to him, maybe they were. With a sudden flash of inspiration, maybe the closest I've ever come to a smart retort, I dropped the needle back on the song I'd just been listening to, O. V. Wright's version of Latimore's brilliant 'Let's Straighten it Out', and the jazz guy gave a smile which acknowledged temporary defeat and apology. He smiled because 'Let's Straighten it Out' is about as far as you can get from teen music without actually wheeling in Miles Davis or Von Karajan. It begins with a little dark, bluesy piano solo that immediately sets a tone of unambiguous seriousness, and the lyric is about sitting down and attempting to sort out what would appear to be grave problems in a well-established relationship, perhaps even a marriage, for God's sake, and it's sung by a man in his late forties or early fifties who has terrible dental problems (really – his teeth whistle at inopportune moments). This could only be mistaken for kids' stuff if you were of the opinion that anything that comes in at under symphony length and that involves a verse, a chorus and a drummer is kids' stuff. I loved black music for all sorts of reasons, but its desire to pitch for listeners that might have spouses, mistresses, jobs – children, even – was certainly one of them, especially at that moment.

In the end, black music changed, to reflect a new set of values and concerns, and to include a generation that didn't want to listen to a man with chronic dental problems; old-school soul, like the blues a couple of generations previously, had started to sound creaky. (Just as I got to the right age – the age when songs about sitting down and sorting things out would really mean something to me – people stopped writing them.) 'My music is not for you. It's not for anyone over thirty,' rapper Biggie Smalls told his mother before he was murdered, when she complained about the profanity of his rhymes; meanwhile the unthinkable has happened, and white pop artists are trying to make music for grown-ups. Bonnie Raitt sings songs about the biological clock; Elvis Costello, Neil Young, Loudon Wainwright, Dylan, Springsteen and Tom Waits, among others, have all made good albums in recent years which acknowledge both their own and their audience's middle-age. But all this is new for white rock music, which is trying to work out how it can articulate wisdom and maturity (there is still a sense that it wasn't supposed to last this long); I'd still use black music to silence someone who didn't believe that pop music was of any use to adults. D'Angelo is a young man, but 'Playa Playa', the first track on his *Voodoo* album, sounds effort-lessly ripe – unhurried, richly textured, thick as treacle. And while people like him are still making music which sounds like that, I won't be needing jazz for a while yet.

Röyksopp's Night Out
Röyksopp

28

Just as some of us were beginning to fear that club culture was finally going to make us feel excluded from the young person's party (and, let's face it, it was about time), they invented chillout music, and we felt right at home again. Tasteful, quiet people like Zero 7, Gotan Project, and Röyksopp may well provide balm to those who've just come back from a wild, drug-fuelled Saturday night, but the risk they therefore run is that they will also provide balm to those who've had a tough week in the ad agency or the lecture theatre.

I played Röyksopp during idle moments for a couple of months at the end of 2001; my favourite track was 'Röyksopp's Night Out', which had a little more drive to it than the dreamy cuts elsewhere on the album. (I'm afraid I don't do quite enough to feel the need for ambient relief.) However, just as I had decided that 'Röyksopp's Night Out' was a Good Thing – or at least an OK Thing – I started to hear it everywhere. The BBC began to use it as background music when they trailed forthcoming programmes. It was playing in the foyer of an excruciatingly fashionable hotel, where I was waiting to meet an American friend. It was playing in The Body Shop when I went to buy some shower gel. It had, in other words, become a cliché, lazy shorthand for a sort of vacuous monied hip, probably within two or three months of its release, and I couldn't bring myself to play it again.

But that's what happens now: pop music is everywhere. If you like a song, then so, almost certainly, will someone just like you who works on TV advertisements, or in movies, or who edits sports-highlights packages, or puts together compilations for hotels, or chain-stores, or airlines, or coffee shops. (A couple of months before the Röyksopp débâcle, I'd discovered an album by a good and, I thought, impeccably obscure singer-songwriter called Matthew Ryan; I promptly heard the album's best track during my next three straight visits to Starbucks. So he was dead in the water too, or at least drowned in latte.) How is it possible to love or connect to music that is as omnipresent as carbon monoxide?

This may partly explain the teenage fondness for the profanities and antisocial attitudes of hip-hop: neither Starbucks nor The Body Shop nor the Hotel Minimalist wishes to assault their valued customers with obscene raps about Uzis and pussy set to beats that attempt to remove part of your skull, thus allowing contemporary youth to bond with their favourite artists in private. I was able to do that with Led Zeppelin because no one else was interested: you never heard 'Dazed and Confused' on TV, or in department stores, or in pubs, or even on the radio very often; there was only one TV programme dedicated to the music I liked in Britain. (Now there's probably a 'Dazed and Confused' cable channel somewhere that plays the song twenty-four hours a day.) I was therefore able to foster the notion that Zeppelin were something special, a secret between me and my friends. Such is pop music's current tyranny that it must be almost impossible for kids to think that major artists are speaking directly and intimately to them – how is that possible, when those same artists are speaking to everyone who buys peppermint foot-lotion, or eats at Pizza Hut? The simplest retort to this ubiquity is to listen to and learn to like music that is essentially dislikeable, stuff that would bring the Starbucks compilation people to their knees begging for mercy. You can't sell peppermint foot-lotion with death metal or obscene gangsta rap; you can't use electronic hardcore to entertain passengers waiting for a plane to take off.

So that's the kids sorted: they can listen to stuff that will make their ears bleed and turn their souls black, and good luck to them. But what about us? What can I connect to that I'm not going to get sick of within weeks, that isn't going to have its melodic weaknesses and lyrical banalities exposed by a Renault ad? It seems to me that, for my generation, country music serves the same function as death metal does for people thirty years younger: a pedal steel and a waltz time can still strike fear in the hearts of the timid. Country music is too embarrassingly sincere, too respectful of the past, to be absorbed into the year zero of boutique hotel lobbies; all the alt-country bands of the last few years retain just enough soil on their boots to deter most of the people who want to believe that the world is permanently shiny and new. And there will be other musical bywaters and back alleys too – singer-songwriters whose voices are too croaky and whose lyrics are too morose for commercial consumption, bands who want to combine the attitude of the 13th Floor Elevators with Neil

Diamond's melodic sensibilities – so it's not like we'll have to eat country for the rest of our lives; but God knows we need something that isn't going to come apart in our ears through sheer overuse.

29 **Frontier Psychiatrist**
the Avalanches

No Fun/Push It
Soulwax

30

This, then, is the contemporary musical world – a world wherein no one plays or sings a note, but where new music is indisputably and unambiguously created nevertheless. I once presumed that nothing good – nothing great, anyway – could come out of the mixing and matching and scratching and cutting and pasting, and this was true while the approach of the cutters and pasters remained essentially plagiaristic: the contribution that, say, Eric B & Rakim made to their version of 'I Know You Got Soul' was minimal – it's Bobby Byrd's bassline and beat that define the track.

And any musical response that you might have to Puff Daddy's 'I'll Be Missing You' is actually a response to The Police's pretty riff. You can admire the taste and the cheek, but not the creativity: to create music – to create any art – is surely to pull something out of thin air, to produce something where there was previously nothing.

But now the cutters and pasters have upped the ante. The Avalanches use so many samples to create something so indisputably their own that to accuse them of plagiarism is pointless: you may as well make the same case against a writer whose books contain words that other writers have used before. The Fugees copy great chunks of Marley and Roberta Flack out into their notebooks, and their achievement is all the smaller because of it: the music is overfamiliar, and in any case they don't do anything with it or to it, they alter neither the flavour of it nor the melodic shape of it, subtly or otherwise, in order to make it become something else. Similarly, when R&B singer Angie Stone borrows the riff from 'Back Stabbers' for her song 'Wish I Didn't Miss You', it strikes me as nothing other than an admission of creative bankruptcy, and a vague hope that someone else's genius – and our recognition of it – will carry her through to the end of the track. Somehow we have managed to convince ourselves that this is simply what happens now, as if expecting a songwriter to write a whole new fucking three-minute tune is square.

But the Avalanches use scraps of things you have never heard in ways that you couldn't have imagined; the result is that they have, effectively, created something from nothing. 'Frontier Psychiatrist' consists of a beat, scraps of dialogue from old movies, a few daft noises, and a horn riff pinched from an old and presumably unfunky Bert Kaempfert record; from this unpromising material the Avalanches have created something that builds to a climax and rocks. (They even manage to find a rhyme in two unconnected lines of dialogue.) It's reminiscent of Peter Bogdanovich's film *Targets*, which was bolted together from, among other things, an old horror movie and a couple of days' work that Boris Karloff owed the producers: there's a similar sense of undaunted resourcefulness, the same determination to make the incoherent cohere – and cohere into something new – through talent and a simple force of will. 'Frontier Psychiatrist' is funny, but also vaguely disquieting, because it creates a mood that you haven't quite heard before (always disorienting in pop music, which you can usually count on for emotional familiarity): Kaempfert's almost comically melodramatic horns mean that there's this weird mock-heroic thing going on, a sort of pomposity that is undercut by the frivolity of the other sounds layered over them, but I'm not sure that this is why the track sounds odd. I suspect that the oddness comes about because, just as robots cannot feel love, music that has been produced from this number of samples cannot yet induce any recognition of mood in the listener. There was, one suspects, no one overwhelming sentiment that inspired it, and no particular response expected; this is music created for the hell of it, and it shows.

This is not to suggest that 'Frontier Psychiatrist' is without merit or achievement, because it's not. Indeed, something that's made with this degree of patience is awe-inspiring, in a way: something like, say, 'Yesterday', which is supposed to have come to Paul McCartney in a dream, and seemed so familiar to him that he thought it must have already been written, seems almost unearned by comparison. But if most music is about self-expression, then the self expressed during its composition and performance is invariably a feeling self (even if that feeling is alienation, or ennui, or confusion) and it's disorienting to hear something as emotionally imprecise as this. Maybe we'll become used to it, and learn how to translate and interpret songs drawn from a bewildering number of sources; or maybe collagistes like the Avalanches will be able to refine their art, and make the music they make fit the moods we know. I kind of hope not, as long as people go on making music the straightforward way.

Meanwhile the bootleg phenomenon, whereby DJs slice a couple of songs lengthways and lay one on top of the other, begins to look like the most cheerfully nihilistic musical movement since punk – although as even punks had the sweetly old-fashioned urge to create their own music, you could argue that they only paid lip-service to the ideals of nihilism. People like Soulwax and Freelance Hellraiser (who fused, with unpredictably brilliant results, Christina Aguilera and The Strokes) are telling us that it's finished; they're using the scraps we have left for firewood, so that we have something to huddle round while the hell of the modern musical world freezes over. I'm not sure I agree with them, but Soulwax's *Too Many DJs* is compulsive listening anyway, and the decision to pair up Salt 'N' Pepa's energy with The Stooges' ferocity was especially smart, a music fan's dream: squashing hip-hop on to garage punk is like those arguments boys used to have about what would happen if Spider-Man and Superman teamed up. If you think about it, bootlegging is more democratic than punk. Yes, we could all go out, steal a guitar and learn our three chords, but most of us would still have sounded more like Ed Banger and The Nosebleeds than The Clash; this way allows those of us who have no talent but love our music nevertheless to create something that sounds great. All you need is software, a pair of ears, and great taste: finally, the true genius that is fandom has been recognized.

Pissing in a River
the Patti Smith Group

31

Patti Smith's show at the Union Chapel in Islington, just down the road from where I live, came at the end of a good week. It was hot, a little island of brightness and warmth in the middle of a grey, wet British summer; I was enjoying my work, adapting a book I loved with a good friend, and we were getting on well and producing something we were proud of; Danny's bad stomach had temporarily cleared up, and he was as sunny as the weather.

And Patti Smith was just great. I hadn't expected much; it was an acoustic show, a fund-raiser for the beautiful chapel, and it featured poetry and an auction (half an hour before hitting a whole series of musical peaks, Smith was attempting to flog off a couple of roof tiles and an auto-graphed drumstick). I had presumed that, at best, there'd be a little flash of phosphorus and we'd be given a glimpse of what made her great, once upon a time. I certainly didn't anticipate seeing a riveting, inspiring, occasionally chaotic performance which never once suggested that Patti's best days were behind her.

One of the things you can't help but love about Smith is her relentless and incurable bohemianism, her unassuaged thirst for everything connected to art and books and music. In this one evening she namechecked Virginia Woolf and Tom Verlaine, William Blake and Jerry Garcia,

Graham Greene and William Burroughs; Peter Ackroyd even got a dedication, a thank you for his biography of Blake and his history of London. (One doesn't want to be snooty, but I'm guessing that you get a shorter bibliography at, say, a Bryan Adams show.) I began this book by writing about 'Thunder Road', and there is a sense in which, despite their collaboration on 'Because the Night', it's right that Springsteen and Smith should be at opposite ends of a book, because there is a sense in which they are at opposite ends of a certain musical spectrum. It is not hard to detect in Springsteen's work or in interviews with him an anxiety about how he earns his living, a constant questioning: Am I entitled to this? Can I represent people while at the same time standing in front of them? How will this look, how do I sound? And these questions are important, at least to him, as maybe they should be to anyone who is paid good money to express themselves, but they can be a little constricting. Smith, meanwhile, clearly doesn't give much of a shit. I don't mean to imply that she is irresponsible – her political engagement is evidence to the contrary, and during the Union Chapel show she rapped hypnotically about the foolishness of a possible war on Iraq – nor that she is self-indulgent (although I heard later of one writer who walked out of the show, appalled by the poetry

– which from a Leavisite point of view is understandable, but which misses the point of Smith as a beatnik, an instigator of Happenings, one of the last keepers of the countercultural flame). It's just that she seems blissfully untroubled about her status as an artist: she just is one, and it requires no further contemplation on her part.

I couldn't remember having heard 'Pissing in a River' before, or if I had, it had made no impression on me. That night, however, as Smith hit the electrifying declamatory climax of the song – 'Everything I've done, I've done for you / Oh, I'd give my life for you' – swaying in the blue light, with the church pulpit and the beautiful stained-glass windows behind her, you could feel the whole audience fall in love with her, and the song, and the evening. It was one of those rare moments – miraculous, in the context of a rock show – which make you grateful for the music you know, the music you have yet to hear, the books you have read and are going to read, maybe even the life you live. You can't ask much more than that of your twenty-five quid (chapel renovations included). And though it's too much to expect an epiphany of this kind on a regular basis, it seems to me a worthwhile thing to pitch for.

It's easy, in fact, to get carried away after an experience like that – to demand Smith's kind of commitment and fiery vision from all music. 'I don't care who you listen to, or how good they are,' you want to say to kids who are about to embark on a lifetime of listening, 'just make sure that whoever it is means it, that they're burning up in their desperation to communicate whatever it is they want to say.' But that's not how popular music always works. Gerry Goffin and Carole King sat in an office in the Brill Building and treated songwriting as a day job; they bashed out 'Up On The Roof' and 'Will You Love Me Tomorrow?' because they needed hit records. And I doubt whether Bjorn and Benny would have self-combusted if 'Dancing Queen' had gone unwritten and unrecorded – it's a great song, but it doesn't sound as though anyone's life depended on it. Pop's indifference to motive and conviction is one of its joys. (And in any case, one can think of dozens of bands or singers whose artistic ambition is boundless, who are almost consumed by the importance of their work, but whose songs stink.)

Even so, listening to 'Dancing Queen' is unlikely to leave you wanting to read, or write, or paint, or go to a gallery, or run fast, and that's the effect Smith had on this member of the audience (and, I suspect, on quite a few others). That kind of inspiration is rare, in any area of the arts. And yet now I see that this book is going to end here – because I wanted to try and surf out on the high I felt during the gig, in another attempt to get music to do something that words can't – I'm a little ambivalent about it: maybe it's a little too High Culture, what with Woolf and Blake and Ackroyd and the chapel and all. Maybe I should close with 'Papa-Oom-Mow-Mow' or 'Surfin' Bird' or 'I Hate You So Much Right Now'. On the other hand, the song was called 'Pissing in a River'; and it was played on guitars, and it lasted four or five minutes, and its emotional effects depended entirely on its chords and its chorus and its attitude. It's a pop song, in other words, and like a lot of other pop songs, it's capable of just about anything.

14

. . . and 14 albums

It's a Mann's World:
Melodies for a Darker Mood
June 2000

Every month, on a page entitled 'All Back to My Place', the English rock magazine *Mojo* asks two or three celebrities about their listening habits. It's an unmissable feature – surely everyone wants to know what Spike Lee's favourite album is (it's a toss-up between *Innervisions* and *What's Going On*, or what Sporty Spice sings in the shower (her own songs, as it happens). This month, Ron Mael, from the campy and slightly annoying seventies art-rock band Sparks, answers the question 'What music are you currently grooving to?' thus:

'Grooving may not be the most precise definition of my connection to my current musical choices since grooving is usually reserved for pop music and it's quite evident that quality pop music is among the dearly departed. So I'm currently "grooving" to Duke Ellington's *Live at Newport*, Prokofiev's *Romeo and Juliet . . .'*

The view is not uncommon, particularly among erstwhile pop musicians of a Certain Age, who seem to have abandoned rock 'n' roll and taken up jazz, or classical music, for reasons I can only guess at: Prokofiev! Ellington! Take that, Hanson and Wu-Tang Clan fans! (One feels an irresistible urge to point out that, even if pop music is 'among the dearly departed', Russian Romanticism isn't really happening right now, either.) But if Mr Mael's view means anything at all, it must be in its assumption that pop music is dead in the way that fiction is supposed to be dead – that both have been superseded by new technologies or by other art forms. Nobody sees pop music (or fiction) as tools of the revolution; no one expects them to change the world.

Meanwhile, good, talented musicians continue to make albums that people continue to listen to and good, talented authors continue to write novels that people continue to read. In the last few months, there has been terrific new music by the Eels, Kelis, Angie Stone, Neal Casal, Magnetic Fields, Michael Penn, Elliott Smith, Fiona Apple, Josh Rouse ... For the most part, this is unshowy, old-fashioned, verse/chorus/verse music, the kind the Beatles or Marvin Gaye or Jackson Browne used to make. All that's missing is the shock of the new – a significant absence, admittedly, but then, if the guitar-based three-minute song is to survive, there is bound to be a period like this one, when it just settles into its skin and becomes a means of expression like any other.

The trouble is that pop doesn't know how to sell itself in this way. Aimee Mann is a fine, occasionally brilliant singer-songwriter, nothing more, nothing less, and this plainness of purpose has cost her dearly over the last fifteen, mostly calamitous, years. During the first stage of her career, her band, 'Til Tuesday, had only one hit, the very eighties synthpop tune 'Voices Carry'. She hated it, took over the band, and, in then making two wonderful Beatles-tinged pop-rock records, *Welcome Home* and *Everything's Different Now* (both bombed), drove it into oblivion. There was then a five-year hiatus before she produced her first solo album, *Whatever*, but just as it was released her record company lost its major distributor; she transferred to Geffen, but it was soon taken over by Seagram, and she ended up having to buy her new recordings back. This resulted in yet another gap, of three years, before the next album. Mann has felt bitter and cursed, and many of her songs are expressions of her anger at the music-business executives who, she believes, have hampered her career. 'All you wanna do is something good,' she sang on the last track of her 1996 solo album, *I'm With Stupid* (the title was itself a sly dig at her employers), 'so get ready to be ridiculed and misunderstood/'Cause don't you know that you're a fucking freak in this world?' Self-pity has rarely sounded so attractive.

Part of Mann's trouble is that, though she writes her own songs and sings them, she is not what we've come to expect a female singer-songwriter to be. She plays guitar, not piano, but she is not one of the lads, like Sheryl Crow; she is outspoken rather than introspective, which means that she has little in common with the Carole King school; and she is much too grown-up and circumspect to want to bare her pain in the way that Tori Amos and Fiona Apple do. Earth mother, rocker, fruitcake – these are the jobs rock music has for white adult women at the moment, and as Mann has shown no interest in applying for any of them (she's had her eye on Paul McCartney's nice, comfortable office for some time), she has found herself marginalized.

Now, suddenly, life is looking up, thanks in no small measure to Paul Thomas Anderson, the director of *Magnolia*, who built a couple of the movie's set pieces around Mann's music, wrote dialogue from the opening couplet of one of her songs, and then handed the soundtrack album over to her. In the liner notes, he explains how, in making the movie, he merely 'sat down to write an adaptation of Aimee Mann songs'. Mann was not, it turned out, as unrecognized and undervalued as she had believed; indeed, she was nominated for an Oscar this year. (She didn't win, of course. Phil Collins did – a hilarious instance of cloth-eared injustice, which is good news for those who love Mann's brand of exquisitely tuneful complaint.) Right on the heels of the *Magnolia* soundtrack, she has another album – like London buses, you wait for three years and two turn up at once. *Bachelor No. 2* was to have been available only on the Internet (such modest hopes being typical of Mann's despair), but the renewed interest in her work is so great that you can now walk into a record store and buy it. What have things come to when the ability to purchase a CD over the counter by one of America's sparkiest musical talents is a cause for celebration?

Bachelor No. 2 is Mann's strongest collection to date: there are at least half a dozen songs here that will wriggle themselves into the part of your brain reserved for tune storage and stay there for many months. Only one, 'Nothing Is Good Enough', seems to deal directly with her professional traumas ('Critics at their worst/could never criticize/the way that you do/No, there's no one else, I find,/to undermine or dash a hope/quite like you'), but her bleak and bracing cynicism about our ability to connect with fellow-humans remains gratifyingly intact. 'Satellite', a beautiful, tired waltz that echoes James Brown's 'It's a Man's Man's Man's World', begins with the line 'Let's assume you were right,' and you can almost hear the strain in her voice: in Mann's world, other people are very much in the wrong. The first lines of 'The Fall of the World's Own Optimist' ('There's no charity in you/and that surprises me') and of 'It Takes All Kinds' ('As we were speaking of the devil/you walked right in/Wearing hubris like a medal') reinforce the impression that Mann's arguments are geometrically unique in possessing only one side.

There are some people who are irritated by Mann's self-righteous sense of grievance – Greil Marcus recently described her as 'still whining after all these years' – but it seems to me that pop music, unlike the music of its elders and betters, is able to provide something for every undignified mood. If Mann's songs are whiny, well, who doesn't feel like whining sometimes? (And Heaven knows they're not the only ones – what is Bob Dylan's 'Positively 4th Street' but one long, glorious unresolved moan?)

Granted, if you could have only one album a year, and the musician who made it had to be democratically elected, you'd probably feel obliged to vote for someone with a sunnier, more emotionally generous disposition than Mann's. But there isn't only one album a year; there are thousands, and most of them are much less rich and thoughtful than this one.

What makes listening to *Bachelor No. 2* such a treat is Mann's sinuous, Burt Bacharach-like melodies and her verbal facility. 'Ghost World' has the kind of lyrics that people don't write very often: simple, direct, sweet, resonant – in other words, proper lyrics, instead of tenth-rate poetry. 'Finals blew, I barely knew my graduation speech/ With college out of reach/If I don't find a job it's down to Dad and Myrtle Beach,' runs the first verse; I've read entire first novels that cover similar territory less effectively. (The song, an achingly pretty lament for a nothing-happening teenage summer, also offers a respite from all the typical Mann finger-pointing.) 'Red Vines', meanwhile, is this year's great lost radio hit. It has everything: a gorgeous, understated guitar intro, a swooping and memorable chorus, a preposterously cute piano outro. The epic 'Deathly', which will be familiar to those who already own the *Magnolia* soundtrack (there are a couple of cross-overs), is the closest

Mann comes to musical grandiosity: Michael Lockwood's almost hymnal guitar solo is the aural equivalent of Paul Thomas Anderson's plague of frogs – mighty, savagely beautiful, and somehow redemptive.

'The Fall of the World's Own Optimist' was co-written with Elvis Costello, who shares Mann's interest in the craft of the song, and who has had his own travails with record companies of late. It seems strange that people like Mann and Costello (whose last studio album was a collaboration with Bacharach) should find themselves huddled together for warmth in this way, when all they appear to want is to write classic, essentially mainstream pop. Who would have thought that music like this would become alternative, when it doesn't have an alternative bone in its body? *Bachelor No. 2* is exhilarating proof that there's lots of life in the old dog yet.

Alternative Earle:
Earle:
The Resurrection of a Great Songwriter

July 2000

There is a duet on Steve Earle's new album, *Transcendental Blues*, entitled 'When I Fall', a simple but rousing paean to a love that has endured hard times, which seems fairly ordinary in its concerns and expression until you realize that the female voice in the song belongs to Earle's sister Stacey. 'All these years I've watched you trip and stumble,' she sings in the second verse. 'There were times when I feared that you were lost.' Those familiar with Earle's story will know that his sister's fears were not baseless, and that watching his every misstep, especially in the first half of the nineties, would have been a full-time job. Earle, who is now forty-five, has already been married and divorced six times (although he has had only five wives, ex-wife No. 4 and ex-wife No. 6 being one and the same), and in 1994 he was convicted and imprisoned for possessing narcotics, a sentence that would ultimately put an end to several years of heroin addiction. During this period, Earle stopped making music altogether. Indeed, such was his plight that he did not even own a guitar. If staying married to Earle is difficult, then staying related to him by blood must have been even harder.

The jail term was followed by a successful rehab program, and since then Earle has scarcely put a foot wrong, give or take the odd failed marriage. The comeback began in 1995, with the triumphant but noticeably contemplative acoustic album *Train a Comin'* (its predecessor, in 1991, was a noisy and noticeably uncontemplative live recording entitled *Shut Up and Die like an Aviator*, and could have been – indeed, effectively was – made by somebody else altogether); it marked the relaunch of what has become one of the most creatively successful careers in contemporary American music. Who else has recorded five good-to-great albums in six years? Even the weakest of them, the occasionally over-earnest *El Corazón* (which begins with an acoustic ballad mourning the death of radicalism), contains a handful of great songs, including 'Telephone Road', which should walk straight on to anyone's compilation tape of thrilling nineties moments. This renewed version of Earle gives every impression of wanting to claw back the years he wasted trying to score dope: apart from the constant recording and touring, he has been teaching the art of song-writing in Chicago and campaigning for the abolition of the death penalty; he has started a record label, E-Squared; signed up bands; produced eight records; written poetry; and completed a collection of short stories. Clearly, Earle felt he had some catching up to do. No one should tell him that he's already caught up – indeed, he probably overtook most of us some time in 1997.

Earle's music is a hybrid of Nashville, folk and rock 'n' roll which, when played by younger bands – Wilco, the Jayhawks, Son Volt – has come to be described as alt- (for alternative) country. Those who have been listening to pop music for a long time might be mystified by the suggestion that there is anything new going on here, because most alt-country music sounds remarkably similar to the music made by the Stones and/or Gram Parsons in the late sixties and early seventies. In fact what it has brought to the party is a renewed interest in the craft of songwriting. There has also been a reawakening of interest, among younger musicians, in the history of American folk music. Wilco, for instance, has been busy contemporizing Woody Guthrie. And Harry Smith's extraordinary, recently re-released *Anthology of American Folk Music*, which Earle has been using as a set text in his songwriting course, has provoked the same kind of awestruck admiration that a different generation of musicians held for the Velvet Underground.

Earle has been playing and listening to music long enough that he has no need to graft on roots for his roots rock; the roots are fully established. And just as his last offering, *The Mountain*, was an entirely successful attempt to pay tribute to, and extend the life of, the bluegrass he loves, the new album is a celebration of the pop music Earle has listened to since his childhood and young adulthood. *Transcendental Blues* contains a couple of songs played in the key of Beatles (Earle described recently how a copy of *Revolver* lay on top of a monitor throughout the recording session, like a coded instruction manual), a couple of quasi-Springsteen rockers, and a couple of Dylanesque folk ballads. 'Lonelier Than This' is as pretty as anything Earle has ever written: 'Maybe this is as good as it's gonna get/ And I'll always be this way,' he sings over an impossibly heartsick acoustic-guitar line, and so affecting is the song that you cannot help but wish this kind of ill luck upon him. And the album's closer, 'Over Yonder (Jonathan's Song)', is devastating. It was written for a death-row prisoner, Jonathan Nobles, who was executed by lethal injection in 1998. Earle was present, by Nobles' request, at the execution. Earle's words – mercifully unpreachy, simple, clear-sighted, humane – show an expertise and tastefulness that may surprise those who lost touch with him round about the time he lost touch with himself.

There is an enduring confusion in rock 'n' roll on the subject of authenticity. Those who have lived the sex-and-drugs life, the argument goes, are somehow more likely to speak to us with the voice of wisdom and self-knowledge, but this is rarely the case. There are plenty of screw-ups whose music is trite and shallow, and, besides, this theory of rock is very selective: it is applied to Kurt Cobain but not to, say, Elton John. If you're determined to find Earle's experience audible in his recent music, then, of course, you'll find a line of a lyric here and a rasp in the voice there (the truth is that the rasp is more likely to have been caused by age and tobacco than by heroin, prison, or ex-wives). In *Transcendental Blues* you can hear something about Earle's privations, but authenticists will be disappointed by its obliquity and its lack of luridness. On the sleeve of *I Feel Alright,* the second album since his comeback, Earle tells a little story: 'When I was locked up, I was getting ready to go off on this boy that stole my radio. My partner Paul asked me where I was going. I said, "To get my radio – and then go to the hole for a little while." He looked at me like I look at my thirteen-year-old sometimes, and said, "No you ain't. You're gonna sit your little white ass down and do your little time and then you're gonna get out of here and make me a nice record." SO I MADE TWO.'

In 1941, Preston Sturges made the film of this incident some fifty years before it happened. True, Sturges changed the occupation of the hero from musician to filmmaker and called him Sullivan rather than Earle, but the lessons the two men learn are very much the same: the story of

Steve Earle's post-prison career is of a man who has properly understood the value of music – he remembers how awful it was not to be able to make it (or even listen to it) and everything he has done since has been an attempt to maximize the gift he has for it. In this respect, *Transcendental Blues* is 'about' music much more than it is about heroin addiction or broken marriages. The secret to longevity in the field of popular music, it seems, is to keep listening and to keep learning. Dylan understands this, and Bruce Springsteen does, too; *Time Out of Mind* and *The Ghost of Tom Joad* are the products of people who have been doing some homework. Earle has added Irish music to his tangle of roots – he has been spending parts of the year in Ireland, and *Transcendental Blues* features a song called 'The Galway Girl' – and the freshness and punch of this satisfying collection, its breadth and soul and craft, are the unmistakable sign of someone who takes the simple things in music seriously. No one should underestimate the glee underlying those capital letters at the end of the prison story ('SO I MADE TWO'). Well, with *Transcendental Blues*, HE MADE FIVE.

The latest band signed to Steve Earle's record label, E-Squared, was Marah, a young band from South Philadelphia. Despite its youth, the band knows its music, too: at a recent show in New York it slipped into set covers of 'Come On', by Chuck Berry, the Who's 'Magic Bus', and the Replacements' 'Can't Hardly Wait'. This is a risky strategy, not only because covers can make original material sound awfully thin by contrast but also because the audience may end up feeling as though it were listening to a bar band with no ambition to be anything but a bar band doing covers. Marah, however, remembers that Springsteen's E Street Band was as likely to launch into 'Quarter to Three' at some shows as 'Born to Run', and it never did the group any harm. If you are sufficiently talented (and sufficiently ambitious), then paying tribute to other people's songs can seem more like a way of picking up the baton than of dropping out of the race.

Marah's first album for E-Squared, *Kids in Philly*, shows no shortage of ambition. Like *Transcendental Blues*, it is the product of listening to the right sorts of things – the American canon – without being derivative. But Marah is at a different point in its career; Earle, having lived this music for so long, is able to step outside the great tradition, and be ruminative and reflective. *Kids in Philly* is all urgency, hunger and yearning, and a torrent of words spills all over the tunes with an invigorating disregard for the virtue of economy. (*Kids in Philly* is so urgent that it is only thirty-seven minutes long, which, given the preposterous length of most post-CD albums, is a recommendation in itself.) Despite its banjos and its harmonicas, Marah is much too raucous to be considered anything but a rock band, but its songs are so assured and so exuberantly tuneful – 'My Heart is the Bums on the Street' is just crying out to be covered by Jackie Wilson – that the music turns out to be gloriously inclusive. In the best possible way, Marah sounds as though it wants to be famous. I hadn't realized how much I missed that kind of ambition (most bands squash it flat in case it should make them appear uncool) until I heard it in the band's chord changes and its doggedly starry-eyed backing vocals. It is clear why Steve Earle loves the band, but that kind of hope and ache belongs to another and, one suspects, unhappier time of his life: you might not be able to detect naked pain in the songs of *Transcendental Blues*, but you can spot what that pain has cost him.

3

The Entertainers:
Learning from Los Lobos

April 2001

What a piece of work is a boxed set! How infinite(ish) in faculty! In action, how like an angel! This, at least, is what all serious music buyers tell themselves when they have just spent £30 or more on another impeccably packaged and exhaustively annotated four-to-twelve-disc set. You get home, bursting with anticipation, and sit down to listen to the first half-dozen songs of a beloved artist's recording career, and to read the weighty accompanying essay, and then, somewhere along the line, a vague disappointment kicks in. You become irritated that your favourite song is represented only by a demo or a live recording or an alternative mix that omits the horns. Pretty soon, you find that you're playing only the last few tracks on the second CD –

tracks that you probably already own. A few weeks later, you realize, guiltily, that the fourth CD has not yet been removed from the box, and that it never will be.

There is a reason that the fourth CD is likely to remain unplayed. Boxed sets tell the same story over and over: the artist hits the ground running, perfects a sound, makes too much money, and starts turning out music that is self-parodying or overblown or desperate to latch on to which-ever current musical trend happens to be passing. Enoch Powell once observed something to the effect that all polit-ical careers end in failure, but at least no politician – unlike, say, Rod Stewart – has ever attempted to go disco on us.

I have a very simple, though dismayingly dull, rule governing the purchase of boxed sets: buy only collections by major twentieth-century artists, people whose names you are likely to find in a reputable biographical dictionary. The Dylan Bootleg Series is essential, as are the Ray Charles and Aretha Franklin anthologies on Atlantic – in the last case because the inevitable artistic decline took place at the expense of another record label. The James Brown and Bob Marley boxes describe the invention and sophistication of two hugely important musical genres. As for the rest, however much you tell yourself that you've got to come to grips with the post-Fleetwood Mac career of Stevie Nicks, you'd be better off not forking out that £30.

Nobody would argue that Los Lobos's relatively straight-forward Chicano R&B changed the course of pop-music history. And yet *El Cancionero*, the band's four-CD retro-spective, covering a recording career that has lasted twenty-three years, is a joy from beginning to (almost) end. So much pleasure is rare in collections by far more influential artists (I defy anyone to listen to the Byrds box in its entirety), but the fact that Los Lobos have never really had their moment – at least, not a moment that the world at large might have noticed – says much about what makes this boxed set so appealing. This is not a band that has ever been able to rest on its reputation, much of which has been acquired through the sheer determination to entertain. *El Cancionero* sounds more like a couple of two-hour sets at a wedding reception than like a bid for posterity, and is all the more refreshing for it. That must have been some wedding.

Apart from Steve Berlin, who joined the band in the early eighties, the five members of Los Lobos have been playing together since 1973, when they made a local name for themselves by switching between rock 'n' roll and tradi-tional Mexican music at every community function in East Los Angeles that would have them. Pop music is all about becoming rich and famous in the shortest possible time, but there is something to be said for playing regular gigs at joints like the Red Onion, as Los Lobos did: by the time they began recording, in the late 1970s, they were proficient in ways that their punk peers never achieved. The second track on *El Cancionero*, a bolero entitled 'Sabor a Mí', features deft supper-club-sweet acoustic-guitar solos from three of the band's members. This is not an anthology that begs indulgence for the early years. Los Lobos eventually benefited from the energy of the punk ethic – its earliest rock recordings were for Slash, the legendary LA punk label – but their years at the Red Onion had clearly given them a professionalism that would serve them well.

Los Lobos's full name is Los Lobos del Este (de Los Angeles), a cheeky homage to an apparently cheesy polka band called Los Lobos del Norte. But, if this suggests a certain cool-dude, second-generation irreverence for parental favourites, there is no trace of cheekiness on the opening track of *El Cancionero* – a loving and disarmingly pretty version of 'Guantanamera'. This, though, is the Los Lobos way, and a good number of the eighty-odd songs here are uninflected versions of old *cumbias* and *rancheras* and *corridos* and boleros – even the band's one proper hit recording, a cover version of Ritchie Valens's 'La Bamba', features a refreshingly traditional acoustic exit. Across the Atlantic, and at almost the same time, the young and punk-forged London band the Pogues, who also had an irreverent and culturally specific full name – Pogue Mahone, or 'Kiss my ass' – were similarly intent on disinterring old Irish ballads and rebel songs. The Pogues were musically less accomplished than Los Lobos (although they were fronted by a brilliant, if self-destructive, songwriter, Shane MacGowan), so they contented themselves mostly with giving their Irish heritage a ferocious pounding. Nonetheless, this synchronicity was significant. After fifteen or twenty years of listening to straightforward rock 'n' roll, the pop audience had begun to cast around for new stories, new instrumentation, even new rhythms. In the end, of course, the innovation gets swallowed up by the corporate pop mainstream, which then burps out Ricky Martin, but for a moment it was possible to imagine a polylingual and polyrhythmic future for pop music.

What is striking about the first couple of discs in the *El Cancionero* set is that, although Los Lobos can slip from one musical language into another with admirable ease, these languages never get confused. If 'Guantanamera' is played with a remarkable and un-ironic innocence, then the first original song in the collection, the generic 'We're

Gonna Rock', is as straight-ahead as anything by Jerry Lee Lewis. There is, initially, little interest in cross-pollination. This is one reason why it is perfectly possible to listen to great chunks of the five hours of music on *El Cancionero* without getting sick to death of it – you're getting two bands for the price of one. Oddly enough, it isn't until 1988, when Los Lobos were invited to contribute to Hal Willner's strange and brilliant *Stay Awake,* a collection of Disney songs covered by an eclectic selection of artists (and of interest to your small children only if your small children are fans of Sun Ra and Tom Waits), that something dis-tinctive begins to emerge: the Los Lobos version of 'I Wanna Be Like You', from *The Jungle Book,* is slinky, percussive and funny, and wound over and under those liquid, pretty, and unmistakably Hispanic acoustic guitars is an utterly great and indisputably mainstream American sax solo from Steve Berlin.

Any song in which someone is obliged, as Cesar Rosas is, to sing the line 'I'm the king of the swingers, the jungle VIP' can make only modest claims for itself, but here it sounds like a defining Los Lobos moment. By contrast, 'Will the Wolf Survive?', from the band's first full-length album, sounds like foursquare white rock, with only the faintest pinch of chili.

To point out that there is a clear distinction between two styles of music is not the same as saying that there is a lack of distinction in their execution. I cannot comment with any real confidence on the *cumbias* and the rest; the rock 'n' roll, however, is played with verve, swing and fiery skill. Indeed, there is a moment on the first CD – the electrifying opening to 'I Got Loaded', which sounds like an R&B standard but isn't – when you might find yourself asking whether anyone who has ever been smitten by pop music can fail to have his heart stopped by the chords, the swing and, once again, Steve Berlin's wonderfully greasy sax. I suspect that there is a generation of young people out there to whom 'I Got Loaded' may sound like nothing more than a piece of Gap retro marketing, but the rest of us are likely to hear it as rock's binary code.

The third disc of *El Cancionero* contains several tracks from Los Lobos's richest and most ambitious album, *Kiko*, which is now nearly a decade old. *Kiko* is dressed up in one of classic rock's sharper suits – 'That Train Don't Stop Here' wouldn't sound out of place on one of Van Morrison's deep-grooved R&B albums, and you can hear the Band's facial hair in the stately folk rock of 'When the Circus Comes' – but the instrumentation is more exotic than on anything similar from the same period, and the rhythm section provides a limber funk that is way beyond the grasp of most guitar rock acts. By this stage in their career, Los Lobos had learned how to fuse their two styles. There's nothing quite like the intoxicating 'Saint Behind the Glass', during which a Veracruz harp cascades all over a skiffly bass and drum to create the kind of perfectly measured admixture that the band had been threatening for years.

If *Kiko* marked the peak of the band's career, the descent since then has been gentle, if not quite imperceptible. Only four tracks on *El Cancionero* are taken from Los Lobos's last studio album, *This Time*, and although three of the four are comparable in quality to the music on *Kiko* ('Viking' is heavy-metal anonymous), there is a sense that Los Lobos has arrived at the place they were trying to get to. What you hear now is a band that knows what it wants to play and how to play it, and if that seems too removed from the sound of artistic reach and endeavour, then the remainder of this set is probably not for you. On the evidence of the last CD, the one that, traditionally, never comes out of the box, the members of Los Lobos do not spend much time trying either to re-create youthful glories or to siphon off Mos Def's audience. Nor do they seem baffled as to why they no longer generate quite the same cultural heat that they once did. Instead, they moonlight, in various combinations, on such side projects as the Latin Playboys (sexy, ambient and modern), Los Super Seven (back to the Mexicana), and Houndog (deep blues); make solo albums; and fall into unlikely collaborations (with, among others, Money Mark, of the Beastie Boys). These musicians are not likely ever to be without work. Who else, after all, would be capable of providing covers for tributes to Richard Thompson, Doc Pomus and Johnny Thunders, and then nipping off to record a song for a Robert Rodriguez movie?

El Cancionero ends, bathetically, with a weedy and ill-advised cover of Marvin Gaye's 'What's Going On', some of which is sung with spirit, but no discernible soul, by Sheryl Crow, and it's the only time that the band comes close to pretentiousness or discomfort. The rest of the set sounds like a working band making music that people can use – at weddings, parties, anywhere. Perhaps unwittingly, Los Lobos have stumbled across the secret of the great boxed set: forget about the grand historical statement, and simply make people dance. It is, after all, what the music was invented for.

Sweet Misery:
The Mellowing of Nick Cave

May 2001

It's the sheer ubiquity of pop music that presents such an obstacle to older fans. When I was fifteen, it was satisfyingly hard to hear the music I loved. It wasn't played in supermarkets or on airplanes; it wasn't blasted out of passing cars; there wasn't a TV station devoted to it. In the UK in those pre-promo days, the one rock-oriented BBC programme was so short of visuals that it had to be content with playing album tracks over vintage cartoons. To listen to Led Zeppelin in 1972 I had to be in my bedroom, and I liked it that way. If you are fifteen now, what must it be like for the music you love to be dogging your every step? I don't have the figures to hand, but it seems unlikely that 'Yesterday' received as much exposure during the first five years of its life as the latest Destiny's Child single has in the last couple of weeks.

How, then, given pop music's transmutation into a sort of aural smog, is it possible for an artist to create something that sounds mysteriously compelling? Nick Cave's 1997 album, the austere but haunting *The Boatman's Call*, began with Cave singing, in a lugubrious and irredeemably manly bass, 'I don't believe in an interventionist God.' (In the world of contemporary pop music, there's very little room for theological hesitancy. He's either in or He's out.) It was a first line that conveyed a whole package of messages. The poly-syllabic adjective suggested a certain degree of literacy. (Cave has a published novel, *And the Ass Saw the Angel*, under his belt.) The line also told you, in its introversion and funereal pace, that *The Boatman's Call* was not going to be kids' stuff. If you were feeling gloomy and defeated, then this CD was what you wanted to hear, unless, of course, you take the view that such feelings are best expunged by a bracing dose of Britney. Best of all, these first few bars suggested that here was an artist who was going to inhabit his own world relat-ively undisturbed. The most mournful and misanthropic song on *The Boatman's Call* was entitled 'People Ain't No Good': you knew you were never going to hear it while trying on a pair of jeans or tucking into an Egg McMuffin.

Cave's recordings have always been intense, but they haven't always been quiet. His first successful group, the Birthday Party, made a punk-inspired and self-consciously apocalyptic noise whose main purpose, apparently, was to terrify the audience into submission. When the Birthday Party split, in 1983, Cave (an Australian who, with his pallor and his shock of dark hair, might have helped Tim Burton imagine Edward Scissorhands) formed his current group, the Bad Seeds, whose recordings have become progressively less ragged and scary, without succumbing to the blandness of most adult rock. It's as if the singer had succeeded in converting whatever energy was previously manifested as rage into something no less fierce but much more seductive.

Cave's new CD, *No More Shall We Part*, is, in patches, so transcendentally beautiful that one can be forgiven a small spasm of impatience: if he had this in him, why did he waste all those years shouting at people? (One possible answer may involve drugs; Cave, at an earlier stage of his career, had a much publicized habit, and one or two attendant legal problems.) The opening of the first song on the album, the Victorian-morose 'As I Sat Sadly by Her Side', sounds, with its delicate percussion and ominous strings, like a spooked response to Van Morrison's good-Karma classic 'Astral Weeks', and in white pop you don't get anything much prettier than that.

Unfortunately, the rest of the song doesn't quite live up to the promise of the introduction. More than six minutes long, 'As I Sat Sadly by Her Side' may not be the most protracted pop song ever written, but there is little sense that we are being taken on a musical journey. Cave just ploughs dutifully through one verse after another – the song has no chorus to speak of – as if he were eating an overfilled plate of decent but plain food at a grandparent's house. As a result, one's attention is drawn to the writing, which seems better suited to the nineteenth-century European stage than to a twenty-first-century CD. Try singing along to 'You are not a home for the hearts of your brothers/And God don't care for your benevolence/Anymore than he cares for the lack of it in others.' Cave's stab at a sort of otherworldly timelessness can often result in such ponderous tongue twisters. A song entitled 'Fifteen Feet of Pure White Snow' mentions Matthew, Mark, Mary and the Lord, so when the narrator asks someone to 'put down that telephone', it sounds comically anachronistic; there are very few contemporary rockers who can't pull off a reference to a phone call, but somehow Cave has managed to put himself in that select group.

The title song on the album, however, 'And No More Shall We Part', contains a climax so arresting that the heavy-handedness elsewhere can be rationalized as a risky process of range-finding. The song begins as a resigned hymn to romantic commitment. (Cave, the most ingenuous of confessional songwriters, was recently married, though it's fair to say that you will have heard happier music sung by a newlywed.) Then, suddenly, both the melody line and the focus of the lyric change, and the title now refers to God rather than to a beloved. 'Lord, stay by me/Don't go down/ I never was free/What are you talking about?'

It's a thrilling moment, made more so because, until this point, Cave has held back the album's secret weapon: the heavenly voices of his back-up singers, Kate and Anna McGarrigle. Even the most imaginative dinner-party host wouldn't have seated the ethereal McGarrigles on either side of the hell-raising former Birthday Party singer; their music has a purity that Cave, at one point in his career, would have found laughably prissy. In fact, the combination turns out to make perfect sense. The McGarrigles' second album, *Dancer with Bruised Knees*, is packed with the sort of morbidity that Cave would understand; in any case, the McGarrigles have always sounded as though they'd be more comfortable in an earlier, less comfortable age. At the end of 'Hallelujah', the third offering on Cave's new album, the sisters sing, a cappella, 'The tears are welling in my eyes again/I need twenty big buckets to catch them in,' and you can't imagine that they've ever been asked to do session work as blissfully miserable as this.

In 'The Secret Life of the Love Song', a thoughtful lecture that serves as a preface for his new book, *Complete Lyrics*, Cave describes his love songs as 'gloomy, violent, dark-eyed children' and goes on to compare them to 'lifelines thrown into the galaxies by a drowning man'. The latest addition to this rather tubercular body of work is 'Love Letter', a song as rich and as memorable as anything he's ever produced. The conceit – the narrator says something he regrets and sends a letter to his lover in the hope of repairing the damage – is pop-trite, and despite the Hardyesque pathetic fallacies (wicked winds, skies hanging heavy with rain), the lyrics scarcely bear the weight of Cave's existential despair. The music is another matter – slow, anguished, aching, with the McGarrigles again entering at the song's conclusion to add a heartbreaking shade of blue. In 'The Secret Life of the Love Song', Cave refers to 'what the Portuguese call "*saudade*", which translates as an inexplicable longing, an unnamed and enigmatic yearning of the soul,' but he can't tell us, or other musicians, how you come by *saudade* in the first place.

Nothing else on *No More Shall We Part* is as moving as 'Love Letter', partly because most of the other songs work theatrically rather than musically: it's an experience to wander around the blasted heaths of 'Hallelujah', but it's not going to fit very snugly into the small corners of the average day you might reserve for rock music. 'God is in the House', a small-town satire that Randy Newman might have caught himself whistling, is the closest Cave comes to being merely amusing, but it still contains more savagery than your typical divertissement. 'Homos roaming the streets in packs/Queer-bashers with tyre-jacks/Lesbian counter-attacks,' sings Cave's appalled bourgeois, God-fearing narrator – in other words, another song you wouldn't want to set on Repeat Play.

No More Shall We Part, like so much of Nick Cave's work, is sometimes as unwilling to please and as demanding of your attention as a small child. And yet this may explain why it is such a relief to enter its airless, occasionally over-wrought world. In a time when even the angriest, most intimidating hip-hop or heavy metal seems designed to sell us something – a movie or a wrestling match or a lifestyle – Cave's music doesn't seem remotely interested in selling anything. That is to say, it's music made by an artist, in the old-fashioned, twentieth-century sense of the word. It's not going to make Cave a lot of money, but it's his, and ours, if we want it to be, and for that we should be thankful.

Pop Quiz:
What Does the New
Top Ten List Mean?
August 2001

In 1973, for an essay published in the *New York Review of Books*, Gore Vidal read his way through the *Times* bestseller list in an attempt to understand popular taste, trashing as he passed, among others, Aleksandr Solzhenitsyn and the author of *Jonathan Livingston Seagull*. We have long known that there is a division between literary fiction and the mass market, but it says something about the fragmentation of pop music that there is now some kind of musical equivalent. The *Billboard* charts of top-selling LPs in the month of July 1971 included *Sticky Fingers*, by the Rolling Stones; *What's Going On*, by Marvin Gaye; *4 Way Street*, a live double album by Crosby, Stills, Nash & Young;

Aretha Live at Fillmore West, by Aretha Franklin; and *Mud Slide Slim and the Blue Horizon*, by James Taylor. You can imagine that at the time even the most curmudgeonly critics might have found it in themselves to gush over at least a couple of those. Now, however, in addition to the self-explanatory top-seller charts, we have myriad other lists, from MP3 downloads to top alternative albums to top college, whatever that may mean. (These lists may well have been born of the music critics' despair at popular taste.) There is 'literary', critically approved pop – Lucinda Williams, say, or Wilco, or Nick Cave, none of whom trouble the *Billboard* statisticians much – and the MTV-driven hard rock, rap and R&B that you can find at the front of your local HMV. Some might argue that the critics who wrote about Marvin and Aretha thirty years ago are the very same people who rave about Lucinda Williams today, and they'd have a point: rock critics now seem to have tenure, like senior faculty, which could explain why current youth-targeted music seems relatively unexamined.

I decided, however, that my own lack of familiarity with what people are actually buying in bulk was far too shaming, and so I sat down and listened to the ten best-selling albums in the United States according to the 28 July 2001 issue of *Billboard*. These were, in descending order,

Songs in A Minor by Alicia Keys; *The Saga Continues . . .* by P. Diddy & the Bad Boy Family; *Devils Night* by D12; *Break the Cycle* by Staind; *Survivor* by Destiny's Child; *Jagged Little Thrill* by Jagged Edge; *Take Off Your Pants and Jacket* by Blink 182; *Lil' Romeo* by Lil' Romeo; *Skin* by Melissa Etheridge; and *Hybrid Theory* by Linkin Park. I'd caught a couple of minutes of one of the Destiny's Child videos on TV, but, then, so has everyone who has access to a television. As far as I was aware, I had never previously been exposed to the work of Blink 182, D12, Lil' Romeo, Staind, Alicia Keys, or Linkin Park. In fact, I had to ask myself, Who are these people? What do they sound like? And what's with the numbers in the names?

The single biggest influence on most of these artists, according to the acknowledgements in their liner notes, is . . . Actually, let's see if you can guess. Who do you think is at least partially responsible for such songs as 'Where the Party At', 'Bootylicious', 'Bad Boy for Life', 'American Psycho', 'The Girlies', and 'Pimp Like Me'? Who do you think inspired the rapper on D12's 'Ain't Nuttin' but Music' ('Independent women in the house/Show us your tits and shut your motherfucking mouth' – a chummy reference, presumably, to Destiny's Child, whose hit 'Independent Women Part 1' opens their *Survivor* album)? Give up? OK.

You may well be surprised to learn that the very first person thanked in the liner notes of the CDs containing these gems is the Almighty Himself. He gets thanked on seven of the ten albums, by sixteen different contributing artists. Brian, of Jagged Edge, for instance, declares that without God 'we wouldn't be here doing this third album' – incontrovertible, according to much creationist theory, but a somewhat reductive view of the universe nonetheless. Let's face it, without God the first two albums would have been pretty tricky, too. In a similar spirit, Michelle, of Destiny's Child, is moved to point out to the Creator, 'There is no one like you!!', which is, on reflection, one of the tidiest ontological arguments you could wish to hear.

In fairness, there is very little that would cause offence on either Destiny's Child's *Survivor* or Jagged Edge's *Jagged Little Thrill*. (The hopeless pun on Alanis Morissette's 1995 album *Jagged Little Pill* seems to be an homage to Alanis's ability to sell CDs rather than to her penchant for agonized self-exploration; *Jagged Little Thrill* is not an introspective collection.) There is plenty of cleavage on display on the front of the former, and a lot of tattoos and motorbikes visible on the cover of the latter, but these girls and boys are good-bad, not evil, as the Shangri-Las once put it, and although He might be baffled about what He had to do with any of it, He is unlikely, I think, to get wrathful. This is sweet-natured and competent contemporary R&B, and though it is almost perversely unmemorable – how hard can it be to write one tune that sticks? – and utterly derivative (think girl-power pop soul in the style of the Spice Girls and TLC), you are unlikely to feel the need to call an exorcist if you find copies of either lying around in a teenager's bedroom.

Similarly harmless are the albums by Lil' Romeo and Alicia Keys. Only you will know whether you want to listen to an album by an eleven-year-old rapper. 'It's teenage music, but it's also adult appealing,' the biography on Lil' Romeo's website claims, but this seems extravagantly hopeful, because it's hard to imagine that anyone in his teens would swallow this stuff, and it certainly didn't appeal to this particular adult. The intro features a version of 'Frère Jacques'; track two is effectively a rap version of 'Twinkle, Twinkle, Little Star'; and 'Somebody's in Love' contains the line 'Be my Mickey Mouse, and I'll be your Minnie'. The twelfth track, incidentally, 'When I Get Grown', was written by Lil' Romeo, Master P, PK aka Marcus Carter, Gip Noble, Cecil Womack, Linda Womack, Ahmad Lewis and Stefan Gordy; one or two of these, one suspects, weren't at the very top of their game.

The Alicia Keys disc really isn't bad, however, and is certainly the only album in the Top Ten that I might contemplate playing again one day in the not too distant future, when the memory of this whole *Billboard* experience is a little less ... vivid. *Songs in A Minor*, like a lot of diva R&B, is overproduced and overpolite, and the songs rely too heavily on the groove and on Keys' melisma, rather than on their own structure, but it has its moments – most notably the bluesy, moody 'Fallin'', which borrows liberally from James Brown's 'It's a Man's Man's Man's World', and her cover of a Prince song, 'How Come You Don't Call Me'. Indeed, one of the strengths of the album is Keys' recognition that there was black American music before Whitney Houston. The string arrangements echo Curtis Mayfield, and the occasional willingness to lean on piano and voice suggests that Keys might have come across Roberta Flack and Aretha Franklin.

Politesse comes to seem like the most important and attractive of virtues when you enter the midnight worlds of P. Diddy and D12. P. Diddy's *The Saga Continues ...* and D12's *Devils Night* – like the Staind and Blink 182 albums – come equipped with parental-advisory stickers, and these warnings, let me tell you, mean business. Anyone who has lived through Deep Purple, the Sex Pistols, the Ramones, the Cramps, Grandmaster Flash and Nirvana could be forgiven for thinking that there is nothing out there with the potential to alienate in the way that our music antagonized our parents. We have become accustomed to sonic ferocity (and it was that, as much as anything, that terrified a generation raised on Frank Sinatra and Pat Boone) and to songs that contain every conceivable obscenity, covert and overt endorsement of drug use, and sexually explicit language. Despite all this, an hour in the company of P. Diddy (formerly Puff Daddy, or Puffy, or Sean Combs) is a dismal, sordid experience. We have been told often enough that to disapprove of gangsta rap is pointless, middle class and smug, like disapproving of modern urban life itself. Nevertheless, one is entitled to feel queasy about the enthusiasm for and endorsement of the gangsta life audible on *The Saga Continues* . . . The eponymous first track (the title, as it happens, of the first track on the Jagged Edge album, a coincidence indicative of the general level of self-mythologizing going on at the top of the charts) could, it seems to me, be summarized as follows: some rich, powerful, violent people have been away for a while (who these people are, and where they have been, remains a moot point, particularly since we know enough not to confuse the artist with his narrators), and if, in their absence, you have been trying to muscle in on their turf, then they will not be happy about it. 'Y'all niggaz still talkin? Oh you got a little name little fame little fortune? What you have is a portion/Bout the size of the hats in the back of my Porsche and/So you better use caution.' These rich, powerful, violent people seem to be on speaking terms with people who own firearms; beyond that it is perhaps best not to speculate.

The star of the rap collective D12 is Eminem, who, as some readers may be aware, has caused a stir in the last couple of years, mostly by directing a Tourette's-like and apparently inexhaustible torrent of bile towards his fellow-entertainers, his partner, and members of his family. The D12 album *Devils Night* offers no respite, needless to say; listening to the fourth track here – a 'skit' entitled 'Bizarre', in which one of the gang members' attempts to seduce a colleague's girlfriend goes awry, because he farts all the way through it – was, I think, the single most dispiriting moment of my professional life so far this millennium.

This, of course, is more or less the entire point, and it gives pause. When one is confronted by *The Saga Continues ...* or *Devils Night*, any complacency one might have felt about pop music's no longer having the capacity to alienate or irritate heard-it-all-before liberals evaporates. By comparison, the Sex Pistols' nihilism seems thoughtful and politically engaged. (It came as something of a shock to realize that the music I have been listening to over the past few years is exclusively and disgustingly sensitive. Even my favourite recent hip-hop song, OutKast's 'Ms Jackson', contains the line 'I apologize a trillion times' – a sentiment that would make Eminem gag.) Just about everyone, from the scariest metal singer to the dimmest dance act, wants the world to be a better place, but not Eminem, who veers more towards unmediated hostility and threats of violence, rampant consumerist bragging, casual misogyny and puerility. 'What's going on in the world today? People fighting feuding looting, it's OK/Let it go let it flow let the good times roll,' goes the chorus of D12's 'Ain't Nuttin' but Music'. (The music on *Devils Night*, incidentally, is frequently superb – tense and springy, with a wit and energy that blows P. Diddy's stale, pompous beats away.) The echo of Marvin Gaye is gleefully and knowingly perverse. Eminem must realize that Gaye wanted an answer to the question, and, to the rapper's way of thinking, that kind of political angst is contemptible.

We should have seen this coming. Ever since Elvis, it has been pop music's job to challenge the mores of the older generation; our mistake was to imagine ourselves hipper and more tolerant than our parents. The liberal values of those who grew up in the sixties and seventies constitute an Achilles' heel: we're not big on guns, consumerist bragging or misogyny (where are the people who objected to Bruce Springsteen's use of the phrase 'little girl' when you need them?), and that is the ground on which Eminem and his crew choose to fight. I know when I'm beaten; I can only offer sporting congratulations and a firm handshake.

Blink 182 makes chirpy pop-punk music in the tradition of Green Day and the Dickies, and they have received their parental-advisory sticker for services to grotesque schoolboy humour. (A previous album was entitled *Enema of the State*.) Most of the songs on *Take Off Your Pants and Jacket* deal straightforwardly and unimaginatively with first dates ('First Date') or youthful alienation ('If we're fucked up, you're to blame,' and so on); every now and again, presumably to dispel the air of Monkees wholesomeness, they stick their fingers down their throat and vomit all over their lyric sheet. The chorus of 'Happy Holidays, You Bastard' is as follows: 'Unless your dad will suck me off/I'll never talk to you again/Unless your mom'll touch my cock/I'll never talk to you again/Ejaculate into a sock/I'll never talk to you again.' Why? I don't know why. My copy of the album came with four exclusive bonus tracks, one of which is called 'Fuck a Dog', but maybe I was just lucky.

It is with some relief, then, that one turns to Staind – not because of the music (Staind is a metal band, and can think of no higher calling than to soup up old Black Sabbath riffs), but because at least you know where the group stands. 'Most of you don't give a shit/That your daughters are porno stars/And your sons sell death to kids,' they sing on the very first track. Those of you whose daughters are kindergarten teachers and whose sons sell literary novels in independent bookstores should not take offence. Staind tends to look on the gloomy side, but at least its members care, and their howls of anguish are clearly connecting to the right crowd. One satisfied customer at Amazon.com writes, 'I've had a rough time dealing with abuse, peer pressure, love, rape, hate and self-mutilation' (and although her despair is affecting, is it permissible to wonder whether the self-mutilation at least was somehow avoidable?), before praising the band for providing consolation. Who are we to doubt her? Linkin Park, which performs a similar function to similar acclaim ('One of the best albums of all time by far,' another enthusiastic Amazon customer says of its new album, *Hybrid Theory* – with a bold disregard for the usual mealy-mouthed critical timidity), is a rap-metal band not dissimilar to Limp Bizkit, or, for that matter, to Staind, or to ... Actually, the truth of it is that neither Staind nor Linkin Park nor Limp Bizkit is dissimilar to just about any other band that has played an electric guitar very loud in the past thirty years, which means that there is very little to be said for or about them, though I wish them no ill.

The only album in the *Billboard* Top Ten made by an artist who is forty or older is the one by Melissa Etheridge, and, yes, the music sounds tired, clapped out. Part of this is deliberate – *Skin* is a break-up album, Etheridge's *Blood on the Tracks* – but, in truth, her rock ballads, all throaty vocals and melodramatic chords, do not have the emotional power they might have had fifteen or twenty years ago, and much of the writing here is on the hackneyed side of generic: ' 'Cause you live and you learn/And you learn to hold on/And time will make it heal/And time will make it gone.' It is all obviously the product of personal pain, but this path is rutted with ancient tracks, and, sure enough, Etheridge finds herself trundling along in them. *Skin* is unlikely to remain a bestseller for long, one fears; it's too grown-up, and it's too predictable, and maybe in the *Billboard* universe those adjectives are now synonymous. Sales are no longer the absolute indicator of success or popularity that they once were – this is what we must tell ourselves. The *Billboard* Top Ten means nothing! Kids download everything now! Or they burn CDs for each other! And, yet, hundreds of thousands of young Americans have wanted these albums badly enough to go to a store and spend their cash on P. Diddy and D12 and Blink 182; someone on your street might be listening to 'Fuck a Dog' right now. I shall, when I have recovered my strength, creep back to my little private Top Ten, which consists of penniless artists like the Pernice Brothers and Joe Henry and Shuggie Otis and Olu Dara, who make music full of thoughtful, polite ironies and carefully articulated cynicism and references to our glorious heritage. But I won't kid myself that it's pop music – not any more.

40 Favourite Songs,
2000–2010

Chasing Pavements, Adele

La Realité, Amadou and Mariam

Hope There's Someone, Antony and the Johnsons

You Were Right, Badly Drawn Boy

Bastard, Ben Folds

Mysteries, Beth Gibbons and Rustin Man

Get It Out, Blind Pilot

Mississippi, Bob Dylan

Metarie, Brendan Benson

We Are Nowhere and It's Now, Bright Eyes

Willie Deadwilder, Cat Power

My Favourite Mutiny, the Coup

The Bells Of Harlem, Dave Rawlings Machine

Danko/Manuel, Drive-By Truckers

Red Rover, Fleetwood Mac

I'm Actual, the Format

Great Expectations, the Gaslight Anthem

Look At Miss Ohio, Gillian Welch

Trouble, Inara George

The Trapeze Swinger, Iron and Wine

Love Is a Game, the Magic Numbers

Body, Marah

$20, MIA

Bridging the Gap, Nas and Olu Dara

Sleep All Summer, the National/St Vincent

Love Letter, Nick Cave and the Bad Seeds

Le Vent Nous Portera, Noir Desir

Hey Ya!, Outkast

You Said Something, P. J. Harvey

Such Great Heights, the Postal Service

Chelsea Rodgers, Prince

Don't Feel Right, the Roots

Go or Go Ahead, Rufus Wainwright

This Land Is Your Land, Sharon Jones

and the Dap-Kings

The Underdog, Spoon

John Wayne Gacey, Jr, Sufjan Stevens

She Ain't No You, Thad Cockrell

Here's The Tender Coming, the Unthanks

Kitchen, the Vinyl Skyway

Jesus Etc, Wilco

Discography

Your Love Is The Place Where I Come From,
Teenage Fanclub

If you have no Teenage Fanclub at all, then you might
want to start with *4766 Seconds – A Short Cut To Teenage
Fanclub*, a 2002 compilation that includes both the songs
I write about in this book. They're also both on *Songs From
Northern Britain*, which, if you've already got *Rubber Soul*,
is the next best comfort food you can buy.

Thunder Road, Bruce Springsteen

You know where to get this.

I'm Like a Bird, Nelly Furtado

From the album *Whoa, Nelly!*, which doesn't really offer
anything quite as good as 'I'm Like a Bird'.

Heartbreaker, Led Zeppelin

From *Led Zeppelin II*, the best Zeppelin album for riffs
('Whole Lotta Love', 'The Lemon Song', etc.).

One Man Guy, Rufus Wainwright
From the album *Poses*. 'One Man Guy' is atypical, however: Rufus seems to derive more inspiration from showtunes than from folk or pop, which is fine by me.

Samba Pa Ti, Santana
If you feel compelled to buy a Santana album, then a greatest hits should be more than enough for you. There's one great Santana solo, however, on an album called *Havana Moon*, which I would never have come across had Jerry Wexler not introduced me to it; the song's called 'They All Went To Mexico' (Willie Nelson sings it), and the solo is lovely, disciplined, elegiac and – fear not – short.

Mama You Been On My Mind, Rod Stewart
From the album *Never a Dull Moment*, the one with 'You Wear It Well' on it. Both this and *Every Picture* . . . stand up remarkably well.

Can You Please Crawl Out Your Window?, Bob Dylan
From the album *Biograph*.

Rain, The Beatles

From the album *Past Masters Volume Two*, although
annoyingly you'll probably have all the other tracks –
'Day Tripper', 'Hey Jude', 'Lady Madonna', etc. – worth
having.

You Had Time, Ani DiFranco

From the album *Out of Range*, which contains the lovely
'Overlap'. On most of her albums, however, Ani prefers to
rant and rap, and more power to her – but it seems a little
perverse, given how few people are capable of writing
songs like 'You Had Time'.

I've Had It, Aimee Mann

From *Whatever*, Mann's first solo recording. All her
albums are good (as are the last couple of efforts from
her band, 'Til Tuesday), but on her new one, *Lost In Space*,
her writing seems to have become even sharper.

Born for Me, Paul Westerberg

From the album *Suicaine Gratifaction*. Westerberg's solo stuff is as patchy as his Replacements work, which is one of the reasons why he isn't more famous. There's a worthwhile Replacements anthology called *All for Nothing/ Nothing for All*, and the good songs on that will go some way to explaining the passion of his devotees.

Frankie Teardrop, Suicide

Everyone should listen to Frankie Teardrop once. Get someone who owns Suicide's first album, which is available on CD, to tape it for you.

Ain't That Enough, Teenage Fanclub

See notes for 'Your Love Is The Place Where I Come From'.

First I Look At The Purse, the J. Geils Band

From the album *Full House – 'Live'*, one of the very few records to have survived every vicissitude of my musical tastes.

Smoke, Ben Folds Five
From the album *Whatever and Ever Amen*. I can't believe
the number of reviews I've read which have compared
Folds to either Billy Joel or Elton John; this is obviously
and blatantly pianist.

A Minor Incident, Badly Drawn Boy
From the soundtrack to *About A Boy*. Novel available
now from Penguin Books.

Glorybound, The Bible
You can't find the version I like. There's another version on
an odds-and-sods album called *Random Acts of Kindness*,
but it really doesn't have the same swing. Boo and Neill
can't find the recording I refer to.

Caravan, Van Morrison
From the live album *It's Too Late to Stop Now*. The BBC
once showed a fantastic film of this concert on *The Old
Grey Whistle Test* – someone should show it again.

So I'll Run, Butch Hancock and Marce LaCouture
From the album *Yella Rose*.

Puff the Magic Dragon, Gregory Isaacs
From the album *Reggae for Kids*, which also features a
pretty good 'This Old Man' by Yellowman. If your kids
are listening over and over again to stuff that makes you
want to smash the cassette recorder, then try the Music
for Little People series: there are great kids' CDs by Los
Lobos, The Persuasions, Buckwheat Zydeco, Ladysmith
Black Mambazo, etc.

Reasons To Be Cheerful, Part 3, Ian Dury & the
Blockheads
From the greatest-hits album *Reasons To Be Cheerful*,
which closes with the overlooked and gruffly beautiful
'Lullaby For Frances'.

The Calvary Cross, Richard and Linda Thompson
From the album *I Want to See the Bright Lights Tonight*.
Linda Thompson's 2002 album *Fashionably Late*, her
first recording for seventeen years, is a delight.

Late for the Sky, Jackson Browne
From the album *Late for the Sky*.

Hey Self Defeater, Mark Mulcahy

From the album *Fathering*. This year's top tip, via my friend Dan DeLuca of the *Philadelphia Enquirer*. *The Instigator* by Rhett Miller.

Needle in a Haystack, The Velvelettes

From *The Best of The Velvelettes*. They did the original version of 'He Was Really Saying Something', also on this compilation.

Let's Straighten it Out, O.V. Wright

Available on *The Complete O.V. Wright on Hi Records Vol. 1*, a double CD that is pretty much all good, if you can stand the whistling teeth. You can find Latimore's original version, with its long, moody organ intro, on *Straighten It Out: The Best of Latimore*.

Röyksopp's Night Out, Röyksopp

From the album *Melody A.M.* The Gotan Project's *La Revancha Del Tango* is the best and most innovative ambient album I've heard – even its Starbucks-y ubiquity hasn't entirely ruined it for me yet.

Frontier Psychiatrist, the Avalanches

From the album *Since I Left You*.

No Fun/Push It, Soulwax

From the album *Too Many DJs*, although this particular track is also on a (bootleg?) album called *The Best Bootleg Album in the World . . . Ever!,* which you can find in the better class of independent CD shops.

Pissing in a River, the Patti Smith Group

From the album *Radio Ethiopia. Land* (2002) anthologizes just about everything you'd want – including this track – on a two-CD set.

Picture credits

page 2 Teenage Fanclub, playing live at the launch for *Speaking with the Angel* in April 2001. It was an evening of music and performance at the Hammersmith Palais, with all proceeds from the evening going to The Treehouse Trust. Photo Simon Weller. **page 8** Bruce Springsteen performing live in Amsterdam, 1993. Photo Paul Bergen/Redferns. **pages 18–19** Ridley Road Market, Streets of Dalston, by Cairo Sealey. **page 24** Led Zeppelin performing at Madison Square Garden, New York, 1977. Photo Michael Putland/Retna. **page 30** Photo of Rufus Wainwright by James Burns/ Camera Press. **page 34** Santana performing live in Los Angeles, 1969. Photo Robert Knight /Redferns. **page 38** Rod Stewart in his pyjamas, London 1974. Photo Ian Dickson /Redferns. **page 44** A selection of Bob Dylan album covers: *Bringing it All Back Home*, *Blonde on Blonde*, *Blood On The Tracks*, *At Budokan*, *The Times They Are A Changin'* and *Desire*. Reproduced courtesy of Columbia Records. **page 52** Ani DiFranco, photo by Karen Robinson. The photo was featured on the front cover of Ani DiFranco's album *Like I Said*. Thanks to Righteous Babe Records. **page 62** Paul Westerberg performing live in London. Photo Patrick Ford/ Redferns. **page 70** Suicide performing in New York, 1980. Photo Ebet Roberts / Redferns. **page 77** the J. Geils Band performing in London, 1973. Photo Dave Ellis /Redferns. **page 85** 'Smoke', written by Ben Folds and Anna Goodman, 1997 Sony/ATV Songs / Annabanana Songs BMI. **page 94** Badly Drawn Boy on the roof of the Radisson Edwardian Hotel, Leicester Square, London, taken early summer 2002. Photo by Steve Double. **page 102** The Bible, South Bank, London, late 1980s. Photo Richard Croft/Retna.

page 110 Van Morrison performing live in London, 1996. Photo David Redfern / Redferns. **page 116** Haggle Vinyl, Essex Road, Islington. Photo John Hamilton. **page 122** Danny's tape player, courtesy of Dad. **page 128** Ian Dury and the Blockheads logo, reproduced with thanks to EMI. **pages 136–137** Jackson Browne photographed in an antique Chevy Bel Air, Hollywood, California, in July 1974. Photo Henry Diltz /Corbis. **page 144** Record shop 'Wood', Cross Street, Islington. Photo John Hamilton. **page 151** The Velvelettes in the mid 1960s. Photo Michael Ochs Archive/ Redferns. **page 157** O.V. Wright's album *The Bottom Line* released 1978, featuring 'Let's Straighten it Out'. Reproduced by permission of Cream Records, by courtesy of Demon Music Group Ltd. **page 162** Röyksopp's Svein Berge and Torbjorn Brundtland near Bergen, Norway, just before Christmas a couple of years ago. The photo appears on their 2001 album *Melody A.M.* Photo Marte Rognerud. Thanks to Svein and Torbjorn. **page 169** Stephen and David Dewaele in their favourite record shop in Ghent, Belgium, March 2002. Photo by Eva Vermandel. **page 175** Patti Smith performing live at the Union Chapel in Islington, 2 August 2002. Photo Gordon Comstock. **page 182** Aimee Mann. Photo Anthony St James / Retna. **page 191** Steve Earle. Photo Dennis Kleiman / Retna UK. **page 200** Los Lobos. Photo Glenn A. Baker / Redferns. **page 211** Nick Cave. Photo Simon Leigh / Camera Press.

Every effort has been made to trace copyright holders and we apologize in advance for any unintentional omission. We would be pleased to insert the appropriate acknowledgement in any subsequent edition.

NICK HORNBY

FEVER PITCH

'Tears-running-down-your-face funny … highly perceptive and honest'
Nicholas Lezard, *GQ*

'A spanking 7-0 away win of a football book … inventive, honest funny, heroic, charming' Jim White, *Independent*

'I fell in love with football as I was later to fall in love with women: suddenly, inexplicably, uncritically, giving no thought to the pain or disruption it would bring …'

For many people watching football is mere entertainment; to some it's more like a ritual; but to others, its highs and lows provide a narrative to life itself. For Nick Hornby, his devotion to the game has provided one of the few constants in a life where the meaningful things – like growing up, leaving home and forming relationships, both parental and romantic – have rarely been as simple or as uncomplicated as his love for Arsenal.

Brimming with wit and honesty, *Fever Pitch* catches perfectly what it really means to be a football fan – and in doing so, what it means to be a man.

'Funny, wise and true' Roddy Doyle

read more

NICK HORNBY

THE COMPLETE POLYSYLLABIC SPREE

This is not a book of reviews. This is not a book that sneers at other books. This is a book about reading – about enjoying books wherever and however you find them.

Nick Hornby is first and foremost a reader and he approaches books like the rest of us: hoping to pick up one he can't put down. The Complete Polysyllabic Spree is a diary of sorts, charting his reading life over two years. It is a celebration of why we read – its pleasures, its disappointments and its surprises.

And above all, it is for you – the ever hopeful reader

'A wonderful book – lucid, funny, sharp, truthful, cheeky, erudite, surprise-crammed, and emanating a delicious tang of sophisticated amusement'
Lloyd Evans, *Spectator*

www.penguin.com

He just wanted a decent book to read ...

Not too much to ask, is it? It was in 1935 when Allen Lane, Managing
Director of Bodley Head Publishers, stood on a platform at Exeter railway
station looking for something good to read on his journey back to London.
His choice was limited to popular magazines and poor-quality paperbacks –
the same choice faced every day by the vast majority of readers, few of
whom could afford hardbacks. Lane's disappointment and subsequent anger
at the range of books generally available led him to found a company – and
change the world.

*'We believed in the existence in this country of a vast reading public for intelligent
books at a low price, and staked everything on it'*
Sir Allen Lane, 1902–1970, founder of Penguin Books

The quality paperback had arrived – and not just in bookshops. Lane was
adamant that his Penguins should appear in chain stores and tobacconists,
and should cost no more than a packet of cigarettes.

Reading habits (and cigarette prices) have changed since 1935, but
Penguin still believes in publishing the best books for everybody to
enjoy. We still believe that good design costs no more than bad design,
and we still believe that quality books published passionately and responsibly
make the world a better place.

So wherever you see the little bird – whether it's on a piece of
prize-winning literary fiction or a celebrity autobiography, political tour
de force or historical masterpiece, a serial-killer thriller, reference book,
world classic or a piece of pure escapism – you can bet that it represents
the very best that the genre has to offer.

Whatever you like to read – trust Penguin.

read more
www.penguin.co.uk